GREEK & ROMAN
HELL

HELL-ON-LINE E-BOOKS
Eileen Gardiner, Series Editor

PUBLISHED
Egyptian Hell
Zoroastrian Hell
Ancient Near Eastern Hell
Hindu Hell
Buddhist Hell

FORTHCOMING
Judeo-Christian Hell
Islamic Hell

Greek & Roman Hell

Visions, Tours and Descriptions of the Infernal Otherworld

Edited by
Eileen Gardiner

ITALICA PRESS
NEW YORK USA & BRISTOL UK
2019

SUBJECTS: Hell, Greek Texts, Roman Texts,

ISBN: 978-1-59910-228-3 (hardcover), 978-1-59910-238-2 (paperback), 978-1-59910-239-9 (ebook)

Cover: Orphic lamina. Gold leaf from the Necropolis of Hipponion (now Vibo Valentia), c. 400 BCE. National Archaeological Museum of Vibo Valentia.

For a Complete List of Italica Press Titles
Visit our Web Site at:
www.ItalicaPress.com

CONTENTS

LIST OF ILLUSTRATIONS   VII

WEB RESOURCES   VII

PREFACE   IX

INTRODUCTION   XI
    Underworld Geography and Underworld Creatures   xii
    Passages   xiii
    Waters   xiv
    Fields and Meadows   xv
    Palaces   xvi
    Infernal Creatures   xvi
    Judgment and Punishment   xvii
    Otherworld Guides   xix
    Otherworld Time and Reincarnation   xx
    Texts   xxi
    A Note on Names   xxxix

BIBLIOGRAPHY   XLI
    Sources   xli
    Studies   xlii

1. THE ILIAD by Homer   1

2. THE ODYSSEY by Homer   3

3. THEOGONY by Hesiod   9

4. HYMN TO DEMETER   13

5. THE FROGS by Aristophanes   15

6. ORPHIC LAMINA from Hipponium   25

7. GORGIAS by Plato   27

8. PHAEDO by Plato   33

9. THE REPUBLIC by Plato   37

10. THE AENEID by Virgil   41

11. METAMORPHOSES by Ovid   53

12. MAD HERCULES by Seneca   57

13. VISION OF THESPESIUS by Plutarch   67

14. DESCRIPTION OF GREECE by Pausanius   75

15. THE GOLDEN ASS by Apuleius   79

16. THE TRUE HISTORY by Lucian of Samosata   83

17. MENIPPUS by Lucian of Samosata   85

NOTES   93

GLOSSARY   97

INDEX   113

LIST OF ILLUSTRATIONS

1. Persephone supervising Sisyphus   8

2. Persephone and Hades   12

3. Cerberus guarding the underworld's gates   24

4. Aeacus, Rhadamanthus and Minos   26

5. Harpy with a shade   40

6. Hermes with Eurydice and Orpheus   56

7. Charon ferrying across the Styx   66

8. Charon welcoming a shade   92

WEB RESOURCES

ABOUT GREEK & ROMAN HELL
http://www.hell-on-line.org/AboutGR.html
INTRODUCTION TO THE TEXTS
http://www.hell-on-line.org/TextsGR.html
GLOSSARY
http://www.hell-on-line.org/GlossGEN.html
IMAGES
http://www.hell-on-line.org/ImagesGR.html
BIBLIOGRAPHY
http://www.hell-on-line.org/BibGR.html

PREFACE

This anthology of stories and texts from the Greek and Roman traditions has been compiled to facilitate the study of ancient Western notions of hell. Gathered from a variety of sources, the selections included here provide a basis for a comparative overview of the literature on the otherworld.

This volume includes seventeen works dating from 700 BCE until c. 200 CE, almost a millennium, stretching across the eastern Mediterranean. The introduction contains a discussion and an analysis of the various texts. Also included are a bibliography, glossary, and notes to guide the reader and to provide additional resources.

Once contemporary notions of hell are examined in the light of the texts found in ancient and classical traditions, our understanding of the meaning and sources for Western, and particularly Christian, concepts of punishment in an afterlife can be better understood.

The associated website Hell-on-Line.org provides additional information on hell, its traditions, and texts. The site includes bibliographies, a motif index, and a glossary, as well as other tools to assist readers in understanding the literature of hell, its historic and critical tradition, and its relationship to religious beliefs.

I would like to thank Dr. Anna Maria Rotella for her generous introduction to and help with the Orphic Lamina at Vibo Valentia and to Dr. Marianne Bergeron of the Ashmolean Museum for information on objects in that collection. Thanks also to the University of Bristol's Arts & Social Sciences Library and the university's Centre for Medieval Studies, in particular to Carolyn Muessig and George Ferzoco, for their generosity and support. I would also like to thank the staff of the New York Public Library, Research Libraries. As ever unending thanks to Ronald Musto for always supporting my work in every way.

Introduction

Charidas, what goes on down there?
Deep Darkness.
But what about all those journeys upwards?
All lies.
And Pluto?
A Fable.
Then we really are f****d!

Callimachus, Ep. 15.3

The literary texts of the ancient Mediterranean present a fairly clear picture of an underworld and bear witness to the changes in its nature and purpose. The strong stamp of Hesiod and Homer marks the geography and inhabitants of later underworld descriptions. Plato and the mystery religions leave their mark on the genre, while satirical and comic works provide a totally different perspective on ancient beliefs. Works written during the long interval between the *Iliad* and the *Odyssey* (c. 700 BCE) and the works of Lucian of Samosata (2nd century CE), a span of almost a millennium, show a remarkable consistency in terms of the underworld's physical features and denizens, as a backdrop for significant changes regarding the nature of the soul and thus the fate of the dead in the otherworld.

A culture's notions about its underworld generally can be discovered through a study of archaeological evidence, written documentation, and literary and other sources. Local beliefs revealed in epitaphs, tombs, and grave goods may at times be at odds with the literary sources. For instance, while it is clear that later Roman literary ideas of the underworld corresponded with Greek notions, earlier evidence indicates that existence was envisioned as continuing in another place after death. Interment therefore occurred in decorated and spacious accommodations with generous grave goods as attested by the Etruscan tombs and their contents. These were less grand but comparable to Egyptian burials. Remains, such as wall paintings, can now be found on site in areas in northern Lazio and southern Tuscany as well as preserved in museums in Tarquinia and Rome. Such physical remains would seem to indicate early Roman belief in a netherworld rather than an underworld.

UNDERWORLD GEOGRAPHY AND UNDERWORLD CREATURES

While the following texts can sometimes be confused and contradictory, sometimes even self-contradictory, a comprehensible underworld does emerge from the Greek and Roman sources. We know that one can enter and exit the otherworld from at least four places, one of them in Italy, at Lake Avernus west of Naples; another in Greece, on the southern Peloponnese in Laconia at Taenarus, where Psyche in Apuleius's *Golden Ass* and Hercules in Seneca's *Mad Hercules* enter the underworld; the third, called the Caves of Hades, east of Istanbul, at the Cape of Acherusia, in northwest Asia Minor on the Black Sea; and the fourth Pluto's Gate at Hierapolis, near Pamukkale in southwest Turkey. In the legends associated with Theseus, there are allegedly six entrances along the Saronic Gulf between Athens and Corinth, each guarded by a cthonic guard. According to the medieval Mirabilian tradition, Lake Curtius, located in the Roman Forum, was an opening to the otherworld — a soldier named Curtius rode his horse into this lake in order to close the entry and protect Rome — but no ancient references to this entrance survive.

PASSAGES

Many of the following descriptions note the great distance and vast separation between the land of the living and the land of the dead. Hesiod claims it would take ten days for an anvil to fall from the earth to Hades. While occasionally it is unclear whether a text refers to Hades or Tartarus, since they may at times be used interchangeably, Tartarus — also sometimes referred to as Erebus after the god of darkness — is usually situated below Hades. It might also seem from some descriptions to lie beside it, raising the possibility that ancient otherworld journeys might be lateral rather than standard descents. The mythical location occupied by Tartarus is sometimes referred to as a place where opposites meet. Plato's *Phaedo* (111e1–12a) describes the Earth as a sphere bored through with holes, with Tartarus bored clear through the Earth's center, which clearly contradicts any idea of a flat Earth with hell beneath it. Roman texts often convey the idea of a vast hollow space with a small entryway, referred to in the *Aeneid* and other Latin texts as the jaws of Orcus.

Some descriptions include a long, dark passage between this world and the otherworld, and the first features of note that the dead reach are the Rivers Styx and Acheron, over which the ferryman Charon transports the dead who have been properly buried. According to Virgil, the unburied dead must wait one hundred years before they reach this place. All the dead must carry a coin for their passage, and those few living individuals who travel to the otherworld must bring an extra coin for the return journey. On the other side, the three-headed dogmonster Cerberus, who guards the gates of the underworld, greets those who have made the crossing. Hercules in Seneca's *Mad Hercules* carries no coins, using his lion pelt and club to subdue the dog.

WATERS

The rivers of the otherworld can vary from text to text, but consistently the Styx and the Acheron seemingly form a border between this world and the other. Modern illustrations of the Greek underworld, which are based on ancient texts, vary considerably and may include the Stygian Marsh or Lake, into and out of which all the rivers (except the Lethe) flow, with the Phlegethon flowing down to Tartarus. These illustrations assume that despite consistencies among the surviving texts, Greek beliefs also varied from region to region and from cult to cult.

In the *Phaedo,* Plato assays a consistent categorization of the rivers when he describes how the first, largest and outermost of the four rivers of Hades is Oceanus. Inside this is the Acheron, the river of pain, which is similar in size and location, but flows in the opposite direction. The third, the Pyriphlegethon or Phlegethon, the river of fire, flows between them. Finally, the fourth is the Cocytus, which Plato claims is the same as the Stygian River since it forms the River Styx.

In the *Aeneid, The Frogs,* and *Mad Hercules,* the Cocytus — the river of wailing — and the Styx appear to be distinct. Although in the *Aeneid,* they are related, and in *The Golden Ass* they share the identical source. There is no river named Oceanus: instead in both the *Aeneid* and *The Frogs* there are five rivers: the Styx, the Cocytus, the Phlegethon, the Lethe — the river of forgetfulness — and the Acheron. The Phlegethon is mentioned in these texts as flowing into the Acherusian Lake or into a great burning lake toward the Acherusian Lake, but some texts say that the waters do not mingle and that this river flows down into Tartarus. The Phlegethon described in the *Aeneid* appears similar to the river in the *Golden Ass* where Venus sends Psyche to gather water. There she finds two monsters on either side of a treacherous chasm, but this text says that the Phlegethon flows into the Cocytus and the Styx. *Mad Hercules* distinguishes four rivers: the Styx, the Acheron, the Lethe, and the Cocytus, the last two arising from a single source in an obscure recess in Tartarus.

So over time and from text to text, the rivers change course, name, and location, but clearly these rivers form barriers that must be crossed — as in crossing from the land of the living to the land of the dead — and they become places of danger and even torment as Hades shifts from a neutral space to a land associated with punishment, purgation, and reincarnation.

There are other nameless bodies of water in the Places of Punishment, which appear in later texts. Plutarch's *Vision of Thespesius* includes three pools: one of boiling gold, a second of freezing lead, and a third of rough iron. Lucian of Samosata mentions three rivers in this place: one of slime, one of blood, and one of flame. The Places of Punishment may be distinct from Tartarus, with the former as the destination of those mortals who may be cured of their evil, and the latter for the Titans as well as incurable mortals, but Plato, in his *Gorgias,* claims that all sinners are sent to Tartarus, the incurable for eternity and the curables for one thousand years.

FIELDS AND MEADOWS

The Field of Asphodel, or the Asphodel Meadows, are mentioned in both the *Odyssey* and the *Menippus* of Lucian of Samosata. In Homer, where the otherworld is a neutral habitation for the dead rather than a place of punishment, this is the same destination for all. Later it becomes the destination of those who are neither good nor bad — morally neutral. It lies before the Plain of Judgment. The Fields of Sorrow or Mourning and the Elysian Fields are both mentioned solely in the *Aeneid*. In the first Aeneas meets Dido, and in the second his father Anchises. *Mad Hercules* refers to the Elysian Fields as the ultimate destination of good rulers, but otherwise describes only a foul earth, a stricken land, a place of death, "worse than death itself."

PALACES

The Palace of Hades or House of Hades, the dwelling place of the god Hades and his queen Persephone, is mentioned briefly in the *Iliad* and more fully in Ovid's *Metamorphoses* as the destination for one of Psyche's errands assigned by Venus, where she must petition Persephone for a day's worth of beauty for Venus. Persephone offers Psyche a royal seat and fine refreshments, which she must refuse. *Mad Hercules* mentions refers to the palace as the hall of royal Dis [Pluto], a dwelling place overshadowed by overhanging rocks.

The underworld itself is often referred to as the House of Hades. It is dark and shadowy, full of mist and gloom and sometimes filth, windy and loathsome. The *Iliad* describes gates of iron and floors of bronze, while Hesiod describes gates of bronze and a bronze wall with a triple fence of night.

INFERNAL CREATURES

While sometimes full of abstract evils like Disease, Hunger, Fear, and War, these ills are embodied as well in the monsters and demons of Hades: Harpies, Gorgons, Furies, and a variety of giants. In addition to Cerberus and Charon, Hades and Persephone, all of whom are mentioned in various texts, Pausanias in his *Description of Greece*, includes a demon with skin that is a blue-black, the color of meat flies. His name is Eurynomus, a figure otherwise unknown, and he, bearing his teeth, sits on a vulture skin. He eats the flesh off corpses, leaving only the bones behind.

Mad Hercules includes a large cast of allegorical figures including, Sleep, Famine, Shame, Fear, Murder, Grief, Mourning, Disease, War, and Age.

JUDGMENT AND PUNISHMENT

After their defeat by the Olympian gods, the Titans were consigned to Tartarus. This special section of the ancient underworld was set aside from the neutral dwelling place of the dead, which only later would be divided into separate destinations, where the dead would be consigned to pain or pleasure based on their moral character.

The *Gorgias* of Plato attests to a tradition where the living, dressed in clothes that reflect their position and with witnesses to attest to their character, stood as living mortals to receive an early judgment concerning their fate in the afterlife. This text describes how Zeus overturned this tradition and assigned three judges to evaluate everyone — naked and without witnesses — after death. On the Plain of Judgment, Aeacus from Europe would judge the dead from that region, while Rhadamanthus from Asia Minor would judge the dead from there. If there was any doubt, Minos, also from Asia Minor, would cast his opinion, and the deceased would be marked with a sign and sent to its proper destination. The same judges are mentioned in *Mad Hercules*.

Plato's *Republic* describes how two holes lead from the Plain of Judgment, one to a place of punishment for the wicked and the other to one free of punishment for the good. The *Odyssey*, the *Aeneid*, and the *Menippus* also mention Minos as a judge. A character named

Rhadamanthus is also mentioned in the *Menippus,* but he does not seem to function as the judge Rhadamanthus.

The punishments of humans are seldom specifically described in these texts, although they often revisit or reference those fallen gods, the Titans. Both the *True History* and *Menippus* of Lucian of Samosata, however, mention the crack of whips and the cries of those being punished. *Mad Hercules* mentions immured souls and scourged tyrants.

Although Aristophanes' *The Frogs* is a less-than-serious description of the underworld, it does mention the presence of tens of thousands of snakes and savage monsters who punish various types of sinners. It also mentions the dead thrown into pits, covered with piles of bricks, being hacked, racked, flayed, flogged, and hung and finally having acid stuffed into noses.

Oath breakers and those who lack respect for their parents are specifically singled out for punishment in both Hesiod's *Theogony* and *The Frogs,* while in the *Republic,* Socrates notes that there will be extreme punishment for murders and traitors, those who engage in slavery, those who are impious towards the gods or their own parents, and suicides. In Polygnotus's painting that Pausanias includes in his *Description of Greece,* we witness the punishment of an unfilial son by his father and of a sacrilegious man by a woman skilled in poisons. This text also mentions a monster of the otherworld named Eurynomus who eats the flesh of the dead, but it is unclear whether this is a punishment for sin or simply the usual fate of all the dead. Lucian of Samosata calls out liars (as well as false historians) in his *True History,* and, in the *Menippus,* adulterers, tax-collectors, toadies, informers, millionaires and money-lenders, and those proud of their wealth, lineage, and sovereignty.

Plato's *Republic* clearly describes the purgative power of punishment for those who are curable, if they are not ready for release at the end of one round of punishment.

He narrates how devils bind these shades hand and foot and head, fling them down, flay them and card them with thorns, and then throw them back into the depths of Tartarus until completely purged.

The *Menippus* describes the souls awaiting punishment as stripped naked, hanging their heads in shame. The *Vision of Thespesius* by Plutarch also describes the souls as exposed and naked and goes on to say how they turn themselves inside out to be flayed and cut open by underworld guards. According to Plato's *Republic,* the incurable, on the other hand, were not punished for their own benefit — to purge them of their evil and return them to the cycle of life and death — but tormented and hung up in the infernal dungeon for eternity as a warning for others. In his *Gorgias,* Plato includes among the incurable the sacrilegious, wicked murderers, and the like.

While the *Vision of Thespesius* lays out in detail a three-tiered scheme for the afterlife punishment of those who escape punishment in this life, Virgil's *Aeneid* only alludes to such an arrangement. In Plutarch's scheme, punishment in this world before death might include loss of reputation, and that punishment would alleviate some suffering in the otherworld. Plutarch relates how Swift Poiné is responsible for this type of punishment, while Diké is charged with those who were unpunished for their more difficult crimes in this world and so would require otherworld punishment. The dead are marked by gradients of color, and only when they have been thoroughly purged does the color fade away. Finally Plutarch narrates how the Erinys, or Fates, imprison and exterminate the incurable in cruel and brutal ways.

Otherworld Guides

Although guides would later play a significant role in Christian otherworld literature, the preserved Greek texts generally are for the most part not *catabases* — journeys of a living individual to Hades — where often a guide would be advisable. When the text did involve a journey, advice could be proffered in advance. In the *Odyssey*, Circe advises Odysseus to visit the underworld. The advice he eventually receives from Teiresias concerns his homeward journey. So neither of them act as underworld guides. In *The Frogs*, Heracles advises Dionysus before his descent, but does not accompany him. In the *Vision of Thespesius*, a deceased relative he meets in the underworld, serves more as a tutor on leading a moral life than as a guide to an unknown land. On the other hand, in Roman works, Aeneas does have his Sibyl, Lucian his Nauplius, and Menippus his Mithrobarzanes.

OTHERWORLD TIME AND REINCARNATION

In the *Republic*, Socrates attempts an explanation of the relationship between life in this world and the amount of time between one's death and reincarnation. There is a ten-fold penalty for sins, and these were measured in hundreds of years. Unlike the highly specific times periods designated in Buddhist and Hindu texts, duration of relegation to the underworld is not very cogently laid out here, but from other texts a much simpler formula emerges that seems to consign the dead to the underworld for a thousand years before they are released back into this world, after undergoing a period at the River Lethe where all memory of the past is erased, just as one finds in Buddhist and Hindu descriptions of the otherworld.

While the incurable are never released, even the curable may be sent back to suffer an additional thousand years. in Plato's *Republic*, Er, describes how the mouth of hell will bellow, sounding an alarm, when an incurable or a soul who has not yet completed the specified round of punishment approaches, especially any tyrant. At that point, little savage devils rush out and drag the miscreant back. All the souls, as they approach the mouth of hell expecting release, fear the sound of that bellowing that would summon the devils to prevent their release.

Plutarch's *Vision of Thespesius* describes how souls are generally reshaped for rebirth, although others are returned to their former bodies because of some necessity remaining from their past existence. The *Menippus* tells of a recently passed motion in the otherworld that permits special treatment of rich men who oppress the poor. At death their bodies and souls are separated, and as their bodies are punished in the otherworld, their souls are sent back to earth and placed into donkeys who bear burdens for the poor. They are transmigrated from donkey to donkey for 250,000 years and finally allowed to die.

As time passes, notions of the nature of the underworld and the fate of the dead change. Initially the shades never cease to exist but lose all sense of identity. From the time of Plato and the mystery religions, souls begin to retain memory and identity and eventually either return to this world, losing both memory and identity as they cross the River Lethe, or remain among the blessed in the otherworld. These souls reap benefits from those still living, who are capable of performing beneficial deeds.

TEXTS

The texts presented below are organized according to origin and date, beginning with the earlier Greek texts and following on to the latter Roman texts. These texts include the following.

1. The *Iliad*. In Book 8 of Homer's Greek epic poem, Zeus warns the gods not to involve themselves in the affairs of the Trojan War on the side of either the Greeks or the Trojans. Those guilty of interfering will be hurled into the

deepest pit of Tartarus, as far below Hades as heaven is above the Earth. It is briefly described as having gates of iron and floors of bronze. The gods ignore Zeus's warning, and in Book 20 the turmoil caused on earth reaches the realm of Hades, god of the underworld, who fears that the earth will crack so that all can see his grim, moldy mansions below. Finally in Book 22, Andromache speaks of her dead husband, Hektor, the greatest Trojan warrior, son of King Priam and Queen Hecuba, who has just been killed by Achilles. Even such a noble is destined for the House of Hades under the secret places of the Earth. According to the *Iliad,* Tartarus remains a place for the punishment of the gods, and Hades the dwelling place of dead mortals. The text mentions that the living and the dead can do nothing for each other, a situation that will change over time under the influence of Orphism.

2. The *Odyssey.* In Homer's Greek epic poem, Circe advises Odysseus, the Greek hero of the Trojan War, to visit Hades and seek the blind prophet Teiresias, who will offer him advice on the best way to return to this home on Ithaka. Book 11 describes how the hero cut, flayed, and burned two dead sheep, praying to Hades and Persephone, the god and goddess of the underworld, then waited for Teiresias. He is crowded by the dead attracted by the blood, among them his former companion Elpenor, who recently died on Circe's island. Odysseus is surprised to find him here already, and Elpenor explains that when he fell drunk from a roof, his soul came right down after his body. Eventually Teiresias arrives and explains to Odysseus that his own mother who is nearby will know him if he offers her some of the sheeps' blood, which has the power to restore awareness and speech — some semblance of vitality. Both his mother and Teiresias are surprised to find Odysseus alive and in the underworld, and she explains how it is separated by vast waters, which she calls Okeanos.

When Odysseus is frustrated in trying to embrace her, she explains that the flesh and bones of the dead perish in consuming fire and all that's left is a soul, while another explains that those in Hades are the "silly dead," ghosts who can no longer labor once they reach the meadow of asphodel. He also encounters the ghost of Achilles, praising his son and Minos, son of Zeus, sitting in judgment.

He sees the Titans in their punishments — Tityus, Tantalus, and Sisyphus — as well as Herakles, and finally fearing the arrival of Gorgon, he returns to his ship to sail back across the Okeanos.

Book 24 of the *Odyssey* describes how Hermes leads the suitors of Odysseus's wife Penelope into Hades. As they act like squealing bats, they cross Okeanos and come to Leukas. There they see there many dead Greek heroes from the war.

Hades is depicted in the *Odyssey* as a place far from the living, where souls, who are all equal in death, suffering no punishment or reward, are barely conscious, although they retain both some memory of their past lives and a sense of identity.

3. Hesiod's *Theogony*. This cosmological poem from the first half of the seventh century BCE, details the origins of the gods and their offspring and concerns itself primarily with issues of tyranny and power. He tell of the fate of the Titans, the second generation of the gods, after their defeat by Olympian gods in the ten years of battles known as the Titanomachy or the Titan War. He describes Tartarus as a place as far below the earth as heaven is above it and goes on to elaborate how an anvil thrown down from heaven would take ten days to arrive on earth, the same time it would take the same anvil to travel from earth to the underworld. Unlike Homer's floor of bronze and gates of iron, in Hesiod we find both a fence and gates of bronze,

but also a triple wall of Night. Above this place are the roots of earth and the sea.

Tartarus is windy, loathsome, misty, dank, and gloomy. It is the place where Day and Night alternately meet as one rises and the other sets. Tartarus is guarded by the powerful Hundred-Arms — Cottus and Briareos and Gyes, each with one hundred arms and fifty heads. It is the dwelling place of Night's children, Sleep and Death, where Day never shines. The halls of the underworld are guarded by an unnamed dog [Cerberus] who is friendly to those entering, but refuses to let any leave.

Hesiod goes on the explain that outside Tartarus, perhaps on the same level, is the House of Hades, ruled over by Hades and Persephone. He describes the River Styx as one of the ten rivers of Oceanus, vaulted by high rocks and surrounded by silver pillars in a rugged place. Its cold waters, which flow from a rock, are used for the libations of the gods, but the gods who swear oaths with these waters are severely punished for ten years if those oaths are broken.

4. *Hymn to Demeter.* This Homeric Greek poem, dating between 678 and 625 BCE describes the abduction of Persephone by the god Hades, who is the brother of her mother Demeter and her father Zeus. It describes as well Persephone's annual visit each spring to her mother Demeter in the world of the living, an event marked by the return of fertility to the earth. The underworld is described as the home of Hades and Persephone, a realm of darkness, mist and gloom, the place of the dead, but also a place that serves as a repository of the seeds necessary for rebirth.

In this poem Hades declares that Persephone is worthy of homage and indicates that those who pay homage will enjoy a happier afterlife. It promises the initiates into the Orphic and mystery cults, an alternate and better afterlife than the one awaiting the uninitiated who experience darkness and gloom.

5. *The Frogs*. Aristophanes, the Athenian comic playwright, wrote this play for performance in 405 BCE. It describes the journey of Dionysus, a citizen of Athens, and his servant Xanthias to the underworld to rescue Euripides, since Athens found itself without a decent poet. Before they depart Herakles warns them that the voyage will be perilous as they cross an enormous lake of fathomless depth and a sea of filth and dung. Dionysus construes the warning as Herakles's attempt to deceive him about the underworld. Charon will take Dionysus across in a little boat for two coins, but, Xanthias, not being a free man, is forced to walk around. They are warned that they will see tens of thousands of snakes and savage monsters, who are there to punish a variety of sinners, including oath-breakers and people who abuse their parents and guests, but also those who refuse to pay bought lovers and those who quote a certain bad playwright named Morsimus.

This is the first surviving literary work from Greece to record otherworld punishment of the dead, where conduct determines fate, and some suffer while others do not. It enumerates tortures: being thrown into pits, covered with piles of bricks, being hacked, racked, flayed, flogged, and hung, and finally having acid stuffed into the nose. Because this work is satirical, it is difficult to determine Aristophanes's own views on the behaviors that will result in punishment. His parody is, however, clearly speculating about and articulating certain newly current attitudes.

The underworld is described as a place of sleep and forgetfulness, full of filth and darkness. It is also a place of contrasts: good and evil, sacred and profane, punishment and reward. Mention is made of Empusa — the peg-legged specter with a blazing face — as well as the fierce, multi-headed dog Cerberus — who guards the gates to the underworld — the hell hounds of the River Cocytus, the hundred-headed asp, the voracious sea eel referred to as the Tartesian Lamprey, and the Gorgons from the shores of the Tithrasos River. The judge Aeacus appears as judge.

The geography includes the rivers Styx, Acheron, and Cocytus, as well as inky-hearted rocks and blood-dabbled peaks.

6. Orphic Lamina from Hipponium. This pendant, found in a burial and one of several found in Magna Greca, Thessaly, and Crete, is dated to 400 BCE. Its inscription comprises instructions to the deceased, one initiated into one of the mystery cults — perhaps an Orphic cult — on how to proceed in the otherworld. It guides to deceased to avoid the River Lethe, the river of forgetfulness at the side of a white cypress tree, and to seek a drink instead from the spring of Mnemosyne, the spring of memory. After this the soul will be able to follow the sacred path of the other initiates. The text of this particular lamina, although relatively long, is somewhat corrupt, since the Lethe should be on the left, not the right, and line thirteen is somewhat opaque.

7. *The Gorgias.* Plato's *Dialogue* from c. 380 BCE, features Socrates revealing to Callicles some of the workings of the afterlife with the good being sent to the Isles of the Blessed and the wicked being consigned to Tartarus. This differs from the earlier formula of Hades as destination for all the mortal dead and introduces the element of a judgment on performance in this life to be punished or rewarded in the next.

Socrates explains that in the time of Cronos and even into the reign of Zeus, people, since they had foreknowledge of their impending deaths, appeared for judgment before they died, dressed in their best clothes and accompanied by witnesses to attest to their just life. They were then assigned their destiny by living men.

Pluto and several of the overseers of the netherworld complained to Zeus that the wrong people were being sent to the wrong places, so Zeus revised the procedure. He told Prometheus to end foreknowledge of death among men. Then Zeus required everyone to be judged only after death, naked and without witnesses. He assigned new judges: Rhadamanthus from Asia Minor and Aeacus from Europe each judged the dead from their own regions. When they were in doubt, Minos, also from Asia Minor, would cast his opinion. The place of judgment lay at a meadow where a road forks in two, one leading to the Isles of the Blessed, the other to Tartarus.

Naked, without the signs of rank and status, souls, which had been separated from their bodies, showed all the physical characteristics of the living person, but also showed natural gifts and pursuits. Everything showed: perjury, injustice, falsehood and truthfulness, insolence and debauchery.

This netherworld included the purgative power of punishment for those who were curable. Those who were incurable were punished and hung in the infernal dungeon as an example for others. The judges marked each shade with a sign so those in Tartarus could distinguish the curable from the incurable.

Socrates explains that private persons are usually curable, whereas public persons, especially the powerful — despots, kings, potentates and public administrators — are more likely to be wicked. The powerful good are rare.

8. *The Phaedo.* Plato's *Dialogue* from c. 380 BCE, features Socrates' short disquisition on the movements of waters and wind, the four rivers that flow from earth, winding into and out of the chasm of Tartarus, always flowing in

below where they flow out. The walls of this chasm made it possible to descend only to the center. Beyond that the walls leaned back in over the streams. The first and largest of these rivers is Oceanus, the outermost of the four, which flows around in a circle. The Archeron also flows around in a circle, but in the opposite direction, through desert places into the Acherusian Lake, where most of the dead go for varying lengths of time before being reborn.

The third river, the Pyriphlegethon, flows between the first two and falls into a great burning lake of boiling mud and water. It then proceeds in a circle toward the Acherusian Lake, although their waters never mingle. This river is the source of lava streams. The fourth river is the Cocytus, also known as the Stygian River since it forms the River Styx. It is a wild and awful dark blue water. It flows in the opposite direction from Pyriphlegethon and falls into Tartarus opposite it after they meet at the Acherusian Lake, where it also does not mingle.

Socrates proceeds to explain how these rivers function in relationship to the dead, who from philosophers to tyrants, are led by their genius and sentenced according to the lives they led. Those neither good nor bad are destined for Acheron where they are absolved of wrongs and rewarded for good deeds according to their merit.

Those who number among the incurables — the sacrilegious, wicked murderers, and the like — are sent to Tartarus for eternity. Other wicked people who are capable of cure are also sent to Tartarus, but after a year they are cast out. Murderers are thrown into the Cocytus, while those who sinned against their parents are thrown into the Pyriphlegethon. They flow around toward the Acherusian Lake where they seek forgiveness from those they have harmed. Without forgiveness they are returned to Tartarus to repeat the cycle until they are finally forgiven and can be reborn.

Socrates also mentions those who lived well and how they mount upward after death to live upon the earth as pure beings before they ascend to even better places. He does not describe those places, claiming they are too difficult to explain in the short time that he has. The prospects of punishment or reward in the otherworld are clearly here intended to promote ethical lives in this world.

9. *The Republic.* In Plato's *Dialogue* from c. 380 BCE, Socrates tells Glaucon the story of Er, a bold warrior from the Pamphylian race who was killed on the battlefield. After twelve days as he was about to be cremated on a funeral pyre, he revived to tell what he had seen in the mysterious regions where on either side of judges he saw were four openings: the right two leading up to heaven and the left two leading downward toward Tartarus — one hole each for those going and the other hole for those returning. Er explained that the openings to heaven were clean and pure while their opposite emitted dust and squalor. The judges marked the dead with their destination and sent them on their way.

Er observed that when the souls who entered through the holes came back, they joined together in a meadow encampment. There those from below lamented and bewailed about the dreadful things they had suffered and seen, while those from heaven exclaimed about delights and beauty beyond words.

Socrates attempts to lay out a schema of ten-fold returns for earthly behavior calculating periods of hundreds and thousands of years of suffering or reward. He mentions specific sins that lead to extreme punishment: murder, betrayal, slavery, impiety towards the gods or one's own parents, and self-slaughter. On the other side are rewards for kindness and piety.

Er goes on to tell that mostly he saw tyrants, but there were also those private citizens who had committed great crimes. He mentions in particular the tyrant of Pamphylia, Ardiaeos the Great, who had killed his own father and older brother and committed many other unholy deeds. When Ardiaeos approached the mouth of the underworld to leave, it bellowed, summoning savage men of fiery aspect — little devils — who dragged back Ardiaeos and many like him, who either had not yet completed their punishments or had been designated as incurable. The devils bound these souls hand, foot and head, flinging them down, flaying them, and carding them with thorns. These men told those watching that all tyrants would be thrown back into the depths of Tartarus.

Some of the other souls who had successfully left, explained to Er that everyone feared as they approached the mouth that it would bellow, and they would be dragged back down into the depths.

Neither Er nor Socrates, explains the fate of those released from the holes connecting heaven or the netherworld, although based on the *Phaedo*, they are probably in the meadow awaiting rebirth.

10. *The Aeneid.* Book 6 of Virgil's epic, dating from 19 BCE, tells of Aeneas's journey to the underworld accompanied by the Sibyl. Before he finally encounters his father, Anchises in the Fields of Elysium, he sacrifices four bulls and a ewe and enters a cave that leads through empty realms. Finally they arrive at the entrance to Hades and find arrayed around it Cares, Old Age, Disease, Fear, Hunger, Want, Bondage, Death, Sleep, War, the Furies, and Strife.

At the center of a court they discover an ancient elm where visions hang. Next they pass by monsters — Centaurs, Scylla, Briareos, Chimera, Gorgons, Harpies, and Geryon, but these are all illusions. They next come upon the Styx where the dead await passage over in Charon's boat, but those who remain graveless may wait a hundred years before they journey across. Charon the Ferryman on the Stygian waters warns Aeneas away, refusing to carry the living across. The sibyl, however, is carrying the Golden Bough, and gains a crossing for the Trojan hero in a boat surrounded by ghostly shapes.

Once on the other side, the three-headed dog Cerberus, who guards the entrance to Hades bays at them, and the Sibyl throws him a loaf of honeyed bread that puts the beast to sleep. On his journey toward Tartarus, Aeneas passes the souls of babies at the threshold of Hades, and nearby those who died as a result of unjust judgment. Here Minos sits in judgment of the dead. Aeneas next encounters suicides around whom the Styx winds nine times. In Fields of Sorrow, he finds those who died for love, including his own paramour Dido, who shuns him. On his left a cliff with a high rampart and triple wall is encircled by the Phlegethon. Here where a strong gate and tower is guarded by one of the Furies, he hears sounds of woe and punishment. Here Rhadamanthus punishes those who escaped punishment in this world.

Finally Aeneas comes upon the multi-headed Hydra who guards Tartarus, which unlike Hesiod's calculation, is twice as far below Earth as Heaven is above it. There, in addition to the Titans, he finds those who hated their fathers and their brothers, the greedy and the incestuous, adulterers and traitors.

Aeneas eventually finds his father Anchises, whom he has been seeking, on the plain where the River Lethe flows. While Anchises explains many things to Aeneas about the future of Rome and Italy, he also discusses the Roman belief in transmigration of souls. The souls they can see before them, he tells his son, are due rebirth, and they wait there near the water of forgetting after being scourged of their former sins — hung and stretched and burned until all stain is finally removed. They finally arrive in Elysium, called to the Lethe after 1000 years.

11. *The Metamorphoses.* Book 10 of Ovid's masterpiece from 8 CE recounts the well-known tale of Eurydice and Orpheus, the husband so distraught by the death of his new wife that he travels to the underworld to plead for her release. He finds there a dark and shadowy void beneath the earth where all mortals will eventually come to stay, a place of fear, vast and silent. Orpheus's sorrow is so potent that he stops the normal working of Hades and Tartarus: Tantalus, Ixion, the Belides, Sisyphus, and even the vultures who torment Tityus halt their otherwise ceaseless and obsessive tasks. Even the Furies are silenced.

12. *Mad Hercules.* Seneca's earliest tragedy, a Roman play on a Greek subject, opens as the hero completes the last of the labors set for him by the goddess Juno. Rescuing Theseus from the underworld, Hercules has frustrated the jealous goddess's attempts to destroy him. Act 3 includes Theseus long description of the otherworld from the entrance at Sparta, past the rivers of Lethe and Cocytus to personifications — including Hunger, Fear and War — the Palace of Dis [Hades], and the places of judgment and punishment. Theseus describes Charon the ferryman and Cerberus, the three-headed guardian of the entry to Hades. The Chorus that follows Theseus's dialogue with Amphitryon, the husband of Hercules' mother, continues the description of the Underworld to speculate on the legions of the dead.

13. *The Vision of Thespesius* in Plutarch's *Moralia.* From Greek after 81 CE, this vision of the otherworld, which is strangely similar to later medieval visions, describes the otherworld journey of a profligate and iniquitous man, who falls on his head and appears to lie dead for two days, while his soul travels in the otherworld to receive a warning about reforming his behavior. He returns to this life totally reformed after meeting several relatives

who guide him through the intricacies of the otherworld systems of punishment and reparation.

This work is imbued with Greek mythological figures and Platonic elements. Striking is the description of floating bubbles that burst to release the souls of the dead who congregate together, the good with the good and the evil with the evil. This is very reminiscent of the description of souls in the afterlife found in Bede's *Vision of Furseus*. The underworld itself is thinly described, as a place where the souls can see all around and where stars are widely spread out emitting light in amazing colors and energy that souls can travel along. There are also three pools described, one of boiling gold, a second of freezing lead, and a third of rough iron. The guardians of these pools are like blacksmiths, tossing souls of the avaricious and greedy from one to the other, where they are heated in the gold, frozen in the iron, and embrittled in the lead.

Thespesius, formerly known in this life as Aridaeus, is instructed by a relative he barely recognizes, in the three different sorts of punishment, performed under the watchful eye of Adrasteia, the daughter of Necessity and Zeus. The first under Swift Poiné deals with those who have already in this life received some sort of punishment usually involving a loss of reputation, and only require further emotional purifying. The second group is under Diké who deals with those unpunished in this world for their more difficult crimes and so, exposed and naked, must endure longer and harsher punishment turning themselves inside out as they are flayed and cut open by guards. The third group , under the Erinys, or Furies, the incurable that she exterminates in cruel and brutal ways, are imprisoned in a place with no identity or form.

Thespesius is shocked to meet here relatives enduring punishment, but overwhelmed when his father emerges from a pit marked so that all of his crimes are revealed, because one particular feature of this otherworld is how souls are disfigured with scars and welts according to their wickedness. They are also colored according to the nature of their sins until they undergo sufficient punishment for all their color to attain a unified hue and are finally purified.

The pain associated with these otherworld punishments is described as different in degree from corporeal pain as corporeal pain is from imagined pain. The author singles out for special mention those who leave debts for their descendants who as punishment furiously assault them, covering them like swarming bees. Souls are eventually returned to this life, either twisted or hammered into shape for rebirth. Others are returned to their own bodies as necessitated by their own violence and need for action.

14. *A Description of Greece* by Pausanius. This work includes a description of a painting by Polygnotus (mid 5th century BCE) in Delphi at the Lesche of the Cnidians, which depicts Odysseus's visit to the underworld along with the Fall of Troy. Pausanias attributes the basis for the painting to the *Odyssey* and the unknown *Minyad*. Although the painting described includes numerous mythological figures who dwell in the underworld, description that is relevant to an understanding of Hades are limited to Book 10, chapters 28, 30.6 and 31.10–12.

The painting shows the River Acheron and the ferryman Charon. It depicts two punishments: a man beats his son who failed in proper filial duty and a man guilty of sacrilege is punished by a woman skilled in poisons and other drugs. Another figure named Ocnus is a token of Sloth.

Pausanias mentions details such as Odysseus's companions who carry the sacrificial animals — described as black rams — as well as a group carrying water in jars, where the broken jar of an old woman is interpreted as a sign that she was not a follower of the Eleusian mysteries, so her task in the underworld is condemned to failure.

Three Titans are depicted: Tityus, Sisyphus, and Tantalus. The first is no longer being punished, but continuous torture has reduced him to "an indistinct and mutilated phantom." Sisyphus and Tantalus are still engaged in their endless dooms, with the former pushing his rock uphill and the latter stretching out for food and drink forever beyond his reach. Here his pain is augmented by a rock that hangs overhead ready to crush him.

15. *The Golden Ass* or *Metamorphoses* of Apuleius. Included in this Latin work dating from the late second century CE, is the story of Cupid and Psyche. During the trials of Psyche — after she had violated the strictures set down by Venus — this goddess sends her on two missions to Hades. She is first sent to gather water in a vessel from the source of the Cocytus and the Styx, flowing through a precipitous chasm guarded on either side by unsleeping monsters with long and bloody necks. She is saved by Jupiter, who descends in the form of an eagle to retrieve the water for her.

Venus then sends Psyche a second time into the pit and wrath of hell, this time to bring her back for Venus a day's worth of Proserpina's beauty. Psyche takes herself to a high tower, intending to throw herself down in order to reach Hades, but the tower speaks and advises her how to gain her objective. It sends her to Taenarus in Sparta where she will find an entrance to the underworld. The tower also advises her, as the Sibyl in the *Aeneid* advises Odysseus, to bring two coins, carrying them in her mouth, for the Charon the ferryman and two barley cakes soaked in honey for Cerberus, the three-headed dog. She is also warned of the tricks that Venus has planted: three times she will be asked for help — from a man with a donkey carrying wood, from a man in the Styx with decaying hands, and from three women spinning wool. In helping them, she will drop her cakes and will fail to return from the otherworld.

Psyche finally reaches the palace of Pluto and Proserpina, where the queen offers her a royal seat and delicate meats, but Psyche has been warned to refuse and will accept only a seat on the floor and brown bread. Proserpina rewards Psyche with a box supposedly containing beauty, but when Psyche again fails to avoid the temptation to look, she finds in the box not beauty but infernal and deadly sleep, and she falls to the ground like a corpse.

16. *The True History* of Lucian of Samosata — a second century CE, Greek/Romano-Syrian fictional narrative. In its parody of the fantastic stories included in *The Odyssey*, it describes a visit to the underworld. The narrator is escorted by Rhadamanthus, unidentified — but perhaps the same underworld judge found in other ancient texts — and a ferryman named Nauplius into the place full of the horrible smell of burning bitumen, brimstone, and pitch mixed with the disgusting smell and intolerable fumes of roasting human flesh. Here the air is dark and thick, filled with a pitchy dew. They can hear the cracks of whips and voices yelling. They reach a dry and arid island, stony, rugged, and treeless surrounded by precipitous cliffs. They follow a thorny road until they reach a prison that serves as a place of punishment where the ground is covered with sharp stakes and knife blades, which recalls the knife blades that cover trees found in Hindu and Buddhist hell texts.

There are also three rivers surrounding the prison, the first of slime, the second of blood, and the third, a broad and impassable river of flame full of flaming fish. One bridge crosses all three rivers, and it is guarded by Timon of Athens. In this place the narrator sees the punishment of all types of people from kings to common men, naming only specifically Cinyras, but their guide, who describes all the punishments, explains that the severest torment is reserved for liars and those who write false histories, including Ctesias of Cnidus and Herodotus.

The narrator takes delight in this because, he writes no falsehoods.

17. *Menippus* by Lucian of Samosata — a second century CE, Greek/Romano-Syrian text — satirizes otherworld journeys with its description of Menippus's visit to the underworld. He is guided by Mithrobarzanes, who brings him down the Euphrates on a boat that carries the sacrifices necessary to gain entry to the underworld. They come first upon a woody, deserted, and sunless place, where they dig a pit for slaughtering their sheep and then sprinkle the blood around, while Mithrobarzanes shouts to summon the spirits and the Furies, Hecate, and Persephone. His shouting is so loud, it causes an earthquake that opens the ground, makes Cerberus bark, and frightens Hades himself, as well as Rhadamanthus. They find the lake and river of fire, as well as the Palace of Pluto. Using his lyre, Menippus charms Cerberus into letting them pass by. When they try to cross the lake they find the boat is full of men wounded in the Parthian War, during 161. Charon, thinking Menippus is Hercules, since he carries a lion skin, brings him on board and across, pointing out the way for him.

Mithrobarzanes leads them through the darkness into a large meadow of asphodel until they come to the Court of Minos, who is surrounded by Tormentors, Avengers, and Furies. He will judge the dead, assigning them to punishments that fit their crimes, including the chained group that Menippus sees approaching, a group comprised of adulterers, tax-collectors, toadies, and informers. Another group in neck irons arrives separately made up of millionaires and money-lenders, pale and pot-bellied with each bearing a one-hundred pound "crow" on his shoulders. At this court the shadows of the dead, those that follow everyone along the ground, act as witnesses against the dead. The most harshly punished are those proud of their wealth, lineage, and sovereignty. They are stripped naked and hang their heads in shame, as Menippus taunts those he recognizes.

Menippus notices Dionysius of Sicily who, after being prosecuted by his own shadow and Dion, is about to be chained to a Chimera, but Aristippus of Cyrene saves him after explaining how he was always generous to men of letters.

Menippus next arrives at the place of punishment itself where he can hear the sounds of scourges and the wails of those being punished. He can also smell the reek of burning flesh. He sees racks, pillories, and wheels and how the Chimera tears at the dead as Cerberus ferociously devours them. Here everyone is punished together from kings to slaves, but the poor are punished only half as much as the rich. Menippus recognizes some of the recently dead but they turn away ashamed. Here he also sees the Titans (Ixion, Sisyphus, Tantalus, and Tityus).

Eventually he comes to the Acherusian Plain where he finds the demigods and fair women. The recently dead are recognizable, as well the Egyptians, because of their superior embalming process, but the others are blending together into a moldy, ill-defined, and indistinguishable pile of bones.

As the dialogue continues, Menippus is asked about the fate in the otherworld of those commemorated by great burial monuments. Menippus explains how the greatest are selling salt fish and mending shoes, while philosophers continue as before, cross-examining those they encounter.

He is also asked about a motion that was pending in the otherworld and approved while Menippus was present, which provides for the rich who oppress the poor to have their souls transferred into donkeys for 250,000 years while their bodies are punished in the otherworld.

Finally Teiresias advises Menippus that a simple, common life is the best, and Mithrobarzanes points out a hole through which he can escape back to Greece.

Eileen Gardiner
Bristol, October 2018

A Note on Names

Throughout this book, I have made no attempt to standardize the various forms of different names. Clearly it would be misleading to conflate the Greek and Roman names, so Cupid is Cupid and Eros is Eros. But thus also with Herakles, Heracles, Alcaeus, and Hercules. I have generally followed the choice made by the original translators, hoping that this will convey the diverse usage a reader will encounter when studying ancient texts. The Glossary entries account for all variations, and cross-references are provided there.

BIBLIOGRAPHY

SOURCES

Apuleius. *The Golden Ass*. Trans. by Robert Graves. New York: Farrar, Straus and Giroux, 1998.

Aristophanes. *The Peace, The Birds, The Frogs*. Trans. by Benjamin Bickley Rogers. Cambridge, MA: Harvard University Press; London: William Heinemann, Ltd., 1924. Contains *The Frogs*.

Homer. *The Iliad*. Trans. by Robert Fitzgerald. New York: Farrar, Straus and Giroux, 2004.

Homer. *The Odyssey*. Trans. by Robert Fitzgerald. New York: Farrar, Straus and Giroux, 1998.

The Homeric Hymns. Trans. by Chales Boer. Second rev. ed. Irving, TX: Spring Publications, 1979. Contains "Hymn to Demeter."

Hesiod. *The Homeric Hymns and Homerica*. Trans. by Hugh G. Evelyn-White. Cambridge, MA: Harvard University Press; London, William Heinemann Ltd., 1914. Contains: *The Theogony*; *Hymn to Demeter (Demeter I)*.

Lucian. *Lucian*. Trans. by A. H. Harmon. Cambridge, MA: Harvard University Press, 1926; rpt. 1969. Contains: *Menippus*.

Lucian of Samosata. *The True History*. Trans. by H. W. Fowler & F. G. Fowler. Oxford: Clarendon Press, 1905.

Ovid. *The Metamorphoses of Ovid*. Trans. by Mary M. Innes. Baltimore: Penguin Books, 1955.

Pausanias. *Description of Greece*. With an English Translation by W.H.S. Jones and H.A. Ormerod. 4 vols. Cambridge, MA: Harvard University Press; London, William Heinemann Ltd., 1918.

Plato. *Plato in Twelve Volumes*. Trans. by Harold North Fowler. Intro. by W. R. M. Lamb. Cambridge, MA: Harvard University Press; London, William Heinemann Ltd., 1966. Contains: *The Phaedo*, vol. 1; *The Gorgias*, vol. 3; *The Republic*, vols. 5 & 6.

Plutach. *Moralia*. Ed. by G. P. Goold. Trans. by Phillip H. De Lacy and Benedict Einarson. Loeb Classical Library. London: W. Heinemann; Cambridge, MA: Harvard University Press, 1968. Contains: *Vision of Thespasius*, vol. 7.

Seneca, Lucius Annaeus, and Frank Justus Miller, trans. *Tragedies*. Cambridge, MA: Harvard University Press, 1917.

Virgil. *The Aeneid*. Trans. by Robert Fitzgerald. New York: Vintage, 1990.

STUDIES

Bernabé, Alberto, and Ana Isabel Jiménez San Cristóbal. *Instructions for the Netherworld: The Orphic Gold Tablets*. Leiden: Brill, 2008.

Bernstein, Alan E. *The Formation of Hell: Death and Retribution in the Ancient and Early Christian Worlds*. Ithaca: Cornell University Press, 1993, 19–129.

Bernstein, Neil. *Seneca: Hercules Furens*. London: Bloomsbury Academic, 2018.

Bremmer, Jan M. "Tours of Hell: Greek, Jewish, Roman and Early Christian." In *Topographie des Jenseits: Studien zur Geschichte des Todes in Kaiserzeit und Spätanantike*. Ed. Walter Ameling. Stuttgart: Franz Steiner, 2011.

————. *Initiation into the Mysteries of the Ancient World.* Berlin: De Gruyter, 2014.

Burns, I. F. "Cosmogony and Cosmology (Roman)." In *The Encyclopedia of Religion and Ethics.* Edinburgh: T & T Clark, 1980, 4: 175–76.

Casey, John. *After Lives: A Guide to Heaven, Hell and Purgatory.* Oxford: Oxford University Press, 2009, 65–102.

Edmonds, Radcliffe G. *Myths of the Underworld Journey: Plato, Aristophanes, and the "Orphic" Gold Tablets.* New York : Cambridge University Press, 2004.

Garland, Robert. *The Greek Way of Death.* Ithaca, NY: Cornell University Press, 2001.

Ianelli, Maria Teresa, ed. *Hipponion Vibo Valentia Monsleonis. I volti della città.* Reggio Calabria: Laruffa Editore, 2014.

Janko, R. "Forgetfulness in the Golden Tablets of Memory." *The Classical Quarterly* 34.1 (1984): 89–100.

MacDonald, Ronald R. *The Burial-Places of Memory: Epic Underworlds in Virgil, Dante, and Milton.* Amherst, MA: University of Massachusetts Press, 1997.

Reid, J. S. "The State of the Dead (Greek and Roman)." In *The Encyclopedia of Religion and Ethics.* Edinburgh: T & T Clark, 1980, 11:839–41.

Vielberg, Meinolf. "Omnia mutantur, nihil interit? Virgil's Katabasis and the Ideas of the Hereafter on Ovid's *Metamorphoses.*" In *Otherworlds and Their Relationship to This World: Early Jewish and Ancient Christian Traditions.* Ed. Tobias Nicklas, Joseph Verheyden, et al. Leiden: Brill, 2010, 169–87.

1. THE ILIAD[1]

BY HOMER

Greek, c. 700 BCE

Book. 8.2ff.: Zeus's Warning

Zeus called the gods in council on the topmost crest of serrated Olympus. Then he spoke and all the other gods gave ear. "Hear me," said he, "gods and goddesses, that I may speak even as I am minded. Let none of you, neither goddess nor god, try to cross me, but obey me every one of you that I may bring this matter to an end. If I see anyone acting apart and helping either Trojans or Danaans, he shall be beaten beyond the limits of universal order ere he come back again to Olympus; or I will hurl him down into dark Tartarus far into the deepest pit under the earth, where the gates are iron and the floor bronze, as far beneath Hades as heaven is high above the earth, that you may learn how much the mightiest I am among you."

Book 20.54ff.: The Trojan War Rattles Hades

"Thus did the gods spur on both hosts to fight, and rouse fierce contention also among themselves. The sire of gods and men thundered from heaven above, while from beneath Poseidon shook the vast earth and bade the high hills tremble. The spurs and crests of many-fountained Ida quaked, as also the city of the Trojans and the ships of the Achaeans. Hades, king of the realms below, was struck with fear. He sprang panic-stricken from his throne and cried aloud in terror lest Poseidon, lord of the earthquake, should crack the ground over his head and lay bare his moldy mansions to the sight of mortals and immortals — mansions so ghastly grim that even the gods shudder to think of them. Such was the uproar as the gods came together in battle.

Book. 22.482–85: Hektor's Wife Bids him Farewell

"You are now going into the House of Hades under the secret places of the earth, and you leave me a sorrowing widow in your house. The child, of whom you and I are the unhappy parents, is as yet a mere infant. Now that you are gone, O Hektor, you can do nothing for him nor he for you."

2. The Odyssey[2]

by Homer

Greek, c. 700 bce

Book 11.34ff.: Odysseus Visits the Underworld

When I had prayed sufficiently to the dead, I cut the throats of the two sheep and let the blood run into the trench, whereon the ghosts came trooping up from Erebus — brides, young bachelors, old men worn out with toil, maids who had been crossed in love, and brave men who had been killed in battle, with their armor still smirched with blood. They came from every quarter and flitted round the trench with a strange kind of screaming sound that made me turn pale with fear. When I saw them coming I told the men to be quick and flay the carcasses of the two dead sheep and make burnt offerings of them, and at the same time to repeat prayers to Hades and to Persephone; but I sat where I was with my sword drawn and would not let the poor feckless ghosts come near the blood till Teiresias should have answered my questions. "The first ghost that came was that of my comrade Elpenor, for he had not yet been laid beneath the earth. We had left his body unwaked and unburied in Circe's house, for other labor was pressing us. I was very sorry for him, and cried when I saw him: "Elpenor," said I, "how did you come down here into this gloom and darkness? You have come here on foot quicker than I have with my ship."

"Sir," he answered with a groan, "it was all bad luck of a daimôn, and my own unspeakable drunkenness. I was lying asleep on the top of Circe's house and never thought of coming down again by the great staircase, but fell right off the roof and broke my neck, so my soul went down to the House of Hades."…

Teiresias, with his golden scepter in his hand…knew me and said, "Odysseus, noble son of Laertes, why, poor man, have you left the light of day and come down to visit the dead in this sad place?"...

[Odysseus asks Tieresias,] "I see my poor mother's ghost close by us. She is sitting by the blood without saying a word, and though I am her own son she does not remember me and speak to me. Tell me, sir, how I can make her know me?"

"That," said he, "I can soon do. Any ghost that you let taste of the blood will talk with you like a reasonable being, but if you do not let them have any blood they will go away again."...

I sat still where I was until my mother came up and tasted the blood. Then she knew me at once and spoke fondly to me, saying, "My son, how did you come down to this abode of darkness while you are still alive? It is a hard thing for the living to see these places, for between us and them there are great and terrible waters, and there is Okeanos, which no man can cross on foot, but he must have a good ship to take him."...

Then I tried to find some way of embracing my mother's ghost. Thrice I sprang towards her and tried to clasp her in my arms, but each time she flitted from my embrace as it were a dream or phantom, and being touched to the quick I said to her, "Mother, why do you not stay still when I would embrace you? If we could throw our arms around one another we might find sad comfort in the sharing of our sorrows even in the House of Hades. Does Persephone want to lay a still further load of grief upon me by mocking me with a phantom only?"

"My son," she answered, "most ill-fated of all humankind, it is not Persephone that is beguiling you, but all people are like this when they are dead. The sinews no longer hold the flesh and bones together. These perish in the fierceness of consuming fire as soon as life has left the body, and the soul flits away as though it were a dream."...

The soul of the fleet descendant of Aiakos knew me and spoke piteously, saying, "Odysseus, noble son of Laertes, what deed of daring will you undertake next, that you venture down to the House of Hades among us silly dead, who are but the ghosts of them that can labor no more?"...

The ghost of Achilles strode off across a meadow full of asphodel, exulting over what I had said concerning the prowess of his son.

Then I saw Minos son of Zeus with his golden scepter in his hand sitting in judgment on the dead, and the ghosts were gathered sitting and standing round him in the spacious House of Hades, to learn his sentences upon them.

After him I saw huge Orion in a meadow full of asphodel driving the ghosts of the wild beasts that he had killed upon the mountains, and he had a great bronze club in his hand, unbreakable for ever and ever.

And I saw Tityus son of Gaia stretched upon the plain and covering some nine acres of ground. Two vultures on either side of him were digging their beaks into his liver, and he kept on trying to beat them off with his hands, but could not; for he had violated Zeus's mistress Leto as she was going through Panopeus on her way to Pytho.

I saw also the dreadful fate of Tantalus, who stood in a lake that reached his chin; he was dying to quench his thirst, but could never reach the water, for whenever the poor creature stooped to drink, it dried up and vanished, so that there was nothing but dry ground — parched by a daimôn. There were tall trees, moreover, that shed their fruit over his head — pears, pomegranates, apples, sweet figs and juicy olives, but whenever the poor creature stretched out his hand to take some, the wind tossed the branches back again to the clouds.

And I saw Sisyphus at his endless task raising his prodigious stone with both his hands. With hands and feet he tried to roll it up to the top of the hill, but always, just before he could roll it over on to the other side, its weight would be too much for him, and the pitiless stone would come thundering down again on to the plain. Then he would begin trying to push it uphill again, and the sweat ran off him and the steam rose after him.

After him I saw mighty Herakles, but it was his phantom only, for he is feasting ever with the immortal gods and has lovely Hebe to wife, who is daughter of Zeus and Hera. The ghosts were screaming round him like scared birds flying in all directions. He looked black as night with his bare bow in his hands and his arrow on the string, glaring around as though ever on the point of taking aim. About his breast there was a wondrous golden belt adorned in the most marvelous fashion with bears, wild boars, and lions with gleaming eyes. There was also war, battle, and death. The man who made that belt, do what he might, would never be able to make another like it. Herakles knew me at once when he saw me, and spoke piteously, saying, "My poor Odysseus, noble son of Laertes, are you too leading the same sorry kind of life that I did when I was above ground? I was son of Zeus, but I went through an infinity of suffering, for I became bondsman to one who was far beneath me — a lowly man who set me all manner of labors. He once sent me here to fetch the hell-hound — for he did not think he could find any labor harder for me than this, but I got the hound out of Hades and brought him to him, for Hermes and Athena helped me."

On this Herakles went down again into the House of Hades, but I stayed where I was in case some other of the mighty dead should come to me. And I should have seen still other of them that are gone before, whom I would fain have seen — Theseus and Pirithous, glorious children of the gods, but so many thousands of ghosts came round me and uttered such appalling cries, that I was panic stricken lest Persephone should send up from the House of Hades the head of that awful monster Gorgon. On this I hastened back to my ship and ordered my men to go on board at once and loose the hawsers. So they embarked and took their places, whereon the ship went down the stream of the river Okeanos. We had to row at first, but presently a fair wind sprang up.

Book 24.14 ff.: Penelope's Suitors Are Dispatched to the Underworld

Then Hermes of Cyllene summoned the ghosts of the suitors, and in his hand he held the fair golden wand with which he seals men's eyes in sleep or wakes them just as he pleases. With this he roused the ghosts and led them, while they followed whining and gibbering behind him. As bats fly squealing in the hollow of some great cave when one of them has fallen out of the cluster in which they hang, even so did the ghosts whine and squeal as Hermes the healer of sorrow led them down into the dark abode of death. When they had passed the waters of Okeanos and the rock Leukas, they came to the gates of the sun and the land of dreams, whereon they reached the meadow of asphodel where dwell the souls and shadows of them that can labor no more.

Here they found the ghost of Achilles son of Peleus, with those of Patroklos, Antilochos, and Ajax, who was the finest and handsomest man of all the Danaans after the son of Peleus himself.

They gathered round the ghost of the son of Peleus, and the ghost of Agamemnon joined them, sorrowing bitterly. Round him were gathered also the ghosts of those who had perished with him in the house of Aigisthos.

1.   Persephone supervising Sisyphus pushing his rock in the underworld. Attic Greek black-figure amphora, c. 530 BCE, from Vulci, Etruria (central Italy). State Collections of Antiquities, Munich. (Photo, Bibi Saint-Pol)

3. THEOGONY[3]

BY HESIOD

Greek, 700–650 BCE

And among the foremost Cottus and Briareos and Gyes ravenous for war raised fierce fighting: three hundred rocks, one upon another, they launched from their strong hands and overshadowed the Titans with their missiles and hurled them beneath the wide-pathed earth and bound them in bitter chains when they had conquered them by their strength for all their great spirit, as far beneath the earth as heaven is above earth; for so far is it from earth to Tartarus. For a brazen anvil falling down from heaven nine nights and days would reach the earth upon the tenth: and again, a brazen anvil falling from earth nine nights and days would reach Tartarus upon the tenth. Round it runs a fence of bronze, and night spreads in triple line all about it like a necklace, while above grow the roots of the earth and unfruitful sea.

There, by the counsel of Zeus who drives the clouds, the Titan gods are hidden under misty gloom, in a dank place where are the ends of the huge earth. And they may not go out, for Poseidon fixed gates of bronze upon it and a wall runs all round it on every side. There Gyes and Cottus and great-souled Obriareos live, trusty warders of Zeus who holds the aegis.

And there, all in their order, are the sources and ends of gloomy earth and misty Tartarus and the unfruitful sea and starry heaven, loathsome and dank, which even the gods abhor. It is a great gulf, and if once a man were within the gates, he would not reach the floor until a whole year had reached its end, but cruel blast upon blast would carry him this way and that. And this marvel is awful even to the deathless gods.

There stands the awful home of murky Night wrapped in dark clouds. In front of it the son of Iapetus stands immovably upholding the wide heaven upon his head and unwearying hands, where Night and Day draw near and greet one another as they pass the great threshold of bronze. And while the one is about to go down into the house, the other comes out at the door. And the house never holds them both within, but always one is without the house passing over the earth, while the other stays at home and waits until the time for her journeying comes. And the one holds all-seeing light for them on earth, but the other holds in her arms Sleep, the brother of Death, even evil Night, wrapped in a vaporous cloud.

And there the children of dark Night have their dwellings, Sleep and Death, awful gods. The glowing Sun never looks upon them with his beams, neither as he goes up into heaven, nor as he comes down from heaven. And the former of them roams peacefully over the earth and the sea's broad back and is kindly to men; but the other has a heart of iron, and his spirit within him is pitiless as bronze. Whomever of men he has once seized he holds fast. And he is hateful even to the deathless gods.

There, in front, stand the echoing halls of the god of the lower-world, strong Hades, and of awful Persephone. A fearful hound [Cerberus] guards the house in front, pitiless, and he has a cruel trick. On those who go in he fawns with his tail and both his ears, but suffers them not to go back out again, but keeps watch and devours whomever he catches going out of the gates of strong Hades and awful Persephone.

And there dwells the goddess loathed by the deathless gods, terrible Styx, eldest daughter of backflowing Ocean. She lives apart from the gods in her glorious house vaulted over with great rocks and propped up to heaven all round with silver pillars. Rarely does the daughter of Thaumas, swift-footed Iris, come to her with a message over the sea's wide back. But when strife and quarrel arise among the deathless gods, and when any one of them who live in the house of Olympus lies, then Zeus sends Iris to bring in a golden jug the great oath of the gods from far away, the famous cold water that trickles down from a high and beetling rock. Far under the wide-pathed earth a branch of Oceanus flows through the dark night out of the holy stream, and a tenth part of his water is allotted to her. With nine silver-swirling streams he winds about the earth and the sea's wide back, and then falls into the main, but the tenth flows out from a rock, a sore trouble to the gods. For whoever of the deathless gods that hold the peaks of snowy Olympus pours a libation of her water and is forsworn, must lie breathless until a full year is completed and never come near to taste ambrosia and nectar, but lie spiritless and voiceless on a strewn bed. And a heavy trance overshadows him. But when he has spent a long year in his sickness, another penance more hard follows after the first. For nine years he is cut off from the eternal gods and never joins their councils or their feasts, nine full years. But in the tenth year he comes again to join the assemblies of the deathless gods who live in the house of Olympus. Such an oath, then, did the gods appoint the eternal and primeval water of Styx to be. And it spouts through a rugged place.

And there, all in their order, are the sources and ends of the dark earth and misty Tartarus and the unfruitful sea and starry heaven, loathsome and dank, which even the gods abhor. And there are shining gates and an immovable threshold of bronze having unending roots, and it is grown of itself. And beyond, away from all the gods, live the Titans, beyond gloomy Chaos. But the glorious allies of loud-crashing Zeus have their dwelling upon Ocean's foundations, even Cottus and Gyes; but Briareos, being goodly, the deep-roaring Earth-Shaker made his son-in-law, giving him Cymopolea his daughter to wed.

2.   Persephone and Hades. Greek tondo of an Attic red-figured kylix, c. 440-30 BCE, Vulci(?), Etruria (central Italy). British Museum. (Photo, Marie-Lan Nguyen)

4. HYMN TO DEMETER[4]

Greek, 678–25 BCE

None other of the deathless gods is to blame, but only cloud-gathering Zeus who gave her to Hades, her father's brother, to be called his buxom wife. And Hades seized her and took her loudly crying in his chariot down to his realm of mist and gloom....

Now when all-seeing Zeus the loud-thunderer heard this, he sent the Slayer of Argus whose wand is of gold to Erebus, so that having won over Hades with soft words, he might lead forth chaste Persephone to the light from the misty gloom to join the gods and that her mother might see her with her eyes and cease from her anger....

And Aidoneus, ruler over the dead, smiled grimly and obeyed the behest of Zeus the king. For he straightway urged wise Persephone, saying: "Go now, Persephone, to your dark-robed mother, go, and feel kindly in your heart towards me. Be not so exceedingly cast down, for I, brother to father Zeus, shall be no unfitting husband for you among the deathless gods. And while you are here, you shall rule all that lives and moves and shall have the greatest rights among the deathless gods. Those who defraud you and do not appease your power with offerings, reverently performing rites and paying fit gifts, shall be punished for evermore."...

Happy is he among men upon earth who has seen these mysteries, but he who is uninitiate and who has no part in them, never has lot of like good things once he is dead, down in the darkness and gloom.

5. THE FROGS[5]

BY ARISTOPHANES (444–385 BCE)

Greek, 405 BCE

Cast of Characters (partial)

Xanthias, servant of Dionysus
Dionysus, a citizen of Athens
Heracles
Charon
Aeacus
Hostess, keeper of cook-shop
Plathane, her partner

Heracles: A parlous voyage that,
    For first you'll come to an enormous lake
    Of fathomless depth.
Dionysus: And how am I to cross?
Heracles: An ancient mariner will row you over
    In a wee boat, so big. The fare's two obols.
Dionysus: Fie! The power two obols have, the
        whole world through
    How came they thither?
Heracles: Theseus took them down.
    And next you'll see great snakes and savage
        monsters
    In tens of thousands.
Dionysus: You needn't try to scare me,
    I'm going to go.
Heracles: Then weltering seas of filth
    And ever-rippling dung: and plunged therein,
    Whoso has wronged the stranger here on earth,
    Or robbed his boy-love of the promised pay,
    Or swinged his mother, or profanely smitten

His father's check, or sworn an oath forsworn,
Or copied out a speech of Morsimus.
Dionysus: There too, perdie, should he be
      plunged, whoe'er
Has danced the sword-dance of Cinesias....

Dionysus: Why, that's the lake, by Zeus,
    Whereof he spake, and yon's the ferry-boat.
Xanthias: Poseidon, yes, and that old fellow's
      Charon.
Dionysus: Charon! O welcome, Charon! Welcome,
      Charon!
Charon: Who's for the Rest from every pain and ill?
    Who's for the Lethe's plain? The Donkey-shearings?
    Who's for Cerberia? Taenarum? Or the Ravens?
Dionysus: I.
Charon: Hurry in.
Dionysus: But where are you going really?
    In truth to the Ravens?
Charon: Aye, for your behoof. Step in.
Dionysus: *(to Xanthias)* Now, lad.
Charon: A slave? I take no slave,
    Unless he has fought for his body-rights at sea.
Xanthias: I couldn't go. I'd got the eye-disease.
Charon: Then fetch a circuit round about the lake.
Xanthias: Where must I wait?
Charon: Beside the Withering Stone, hard by the Rest.
Dionysus: You understand?
Xanthias: Too well.
    O, what ill omen crossed me as I started! *(Exit.)*
Charon: *(to Dionysus)* Sit to the oar.
    (calling) Who else for the boat? Be quick.
    (to Dionysus) Hi! What are you doing?
Dionysus: What am I doing? Sitting
    On the oar. You told me to, yourself
Charon: Now sit you there, you little Potgut.

Dionysus: Now stretch your arms full length before you.

Charon: Come, don't keep fooling. Plant your feet. Pull
    with a will.

Dionysus: Why, how am I to pull?
    I'm not an oarsman, seaman, Salaminian. I can't.

Charon: You can. Just dip your oar in once,
    You'll hear the loveliest timing songs....
        (Chrous of Frogs)

Charon: Stop! Easy! Take the oar and push her to.
    Now pay your fare and go.

Dionysus: Here 'tis: two obols.
    Xanthias! Where's Xanthias? Is it Xanthias there?

Xanthias: *(off stage)* Hoi, hoi!

Dionysus: Come hither.

Xanthias: *(entering)* Glad to meet you, master.

Dionysus: What have you there?

Xanthias: Nothing but filth and darkness.

Dionysus: But tell me, did you see the parricides
    And perjured folk he mentioned?

Xanthias: Didn't you?

Dionysus: Poseidon, yes. Why look!
    (pointing to the audience) I see them now.
    What's the next step?

Xanthias: We'd best be moving on.
    This is the spot where Heracles declared
    Those savage monsters dwell.

Dionysus: O hang the fellow.
    That's all his bluff. He thought to scare me off,
    The jealous dog, knowing my plucky ways.
    There's no such swaggerer lives as Heracles.
    Why, I'd like nothing better than to achieve
    Some bold adventure, worthy of our trip....

Xanthias: I know you would. Hallo! I hear a noise.

Dionysus: Where? What?

Xanthias: Behind us, there.

Dionysus: Get you behind.

Xanthias: No, it's in front.
Dionysus: Get you in front directly.
Xanthias: And now I see the most ferocious monster.
Dionysus: O, what's it like?
Xanthias: Like everything by turns.
    Now it's a bull. Now it's a mule. And now
    The loveliest girl.
Dionysus: O, where? I'll go and meet her.
Xanthias: It's ceased to be a girl. It's a dog now.
Dionysus: It is Empusa!
Xanthias: Well, its face is all
    Ablaze with fire.
Dionysus: Has it a copper leg?
Xanthias: A copper leg? Yes, one. And one of cow dung.
Dionysus: O, whither shall I flee?
Xanthias: O, whither I?
Dionysus: My priest, protect me, and we'll sup
        together.
Xanthias: King Heracles, we're done for.
Dionysus: O, forbear, good fellow, call me anything
        but that.
Xanthias: Well then, Dionysus.
Dionysus: O, that's worse again.
Xanthias: *(to the spectre)* Aye, go thy way. O master, here,
        come here.
Dionysus: O, what's up now?
Xanthias: Take courage. All's serene.
    And, like Hegelochus, we now may say
    "Out of the storm there comes a new weather."
    Empusa's gone.
Dionysus: Swear it.
Xanthias: By Zeus she is.
Dionysus: Swear it again.
Xanthias: By Zeus.
Dionysus: Again.

Xanthias: By Zeus.
   O dear, O dear, how pale I grew to see her,
   But he, from fright has yellowed me all over.
Dionysus: Ah me, whence fall these evils on
       my head?
   Who is the god to blame for my destruction?
   Air, Zeus's chamber, or the Foot of Time?
   (A flute is played behind the scenes.)…
Dionysus: What's the right way to knock? I wonder how
   The natives here are wont to knock at doors.
Xanthias: No dawdling: taste the door. You've got,
     remember,
   The lion-hide and pride of Heracles.
Dionysus: *(knocking)* Boy! boy!
   (The door opens. Aeacus appears.)
Aeacus: Who's there?
Dionysus: I, Heracles the strong!
Aeacus: O, you most shameless desperate ruffian, you.
   O, villain, villain, arrant vilest villain!
   You seized our Cerberus by the throat, and fled,
   And ran, and rushed, and bolted, hauling off
   The dog, my charge! But now I've got you fast.
   So close the Styx's inky-hearted rock,
   The blood-bedabbled peak of Acheron
   Shall hem you in. The hell-hounds of Cocytus
   Prowl round you whilst the hundred-headed Asp
   Shall rive your heart-strings, the Tartesian Lamprey
   Prey on your lungs, and those Tithrasian Gorgons
   Mangle tear your kidneys, mauling them,
   Entrails and all, into one bloody mash.
   I'll speed a running foot to fetch them hither.…
   (Exit Aeacus.)
   (Enter Hostess and Plathane.)
Hostess: O Plathane! Plathane! that naughty man,
   That's he who got into our tavern once,
   And ate up sixteen loaves.

Plathane: O, so he is! The very man.

Xanthias: Bad luck for somebody!

Hostess: O and, besides, those twenty bits of stew,
    Half-obol pieces.

Xanthias: Somebody's going to catch it!

Hostess: That garlic too.

Dionysus: Woman, you're talking nonsense.
    You don't know what you're saying.

Hostess: O, you thought
    I shouldn't know you with your buskins on!
    Ah, and I've not yet mentioned all that fish,
    No, nor the new-made cheese. He gulped it down,
    Baskets and all, unlucky that we were.
    And when I just alluded to the price,
    He looked so fierce and bellowed like a bull.

Xanthias: Yes, that's his way: that's what he always does.

Hostess: O, and he drew his sword, and seemed
        quite mad.

Plathane: O, that he did.

Hostess: And terrified us so
    We sprang up to the cockloft, she and I.
    Then out he hurled, decamping with the rugs.

Xanthias: That's his way too. Something must be done.

Hostess: Quick, run and call my patron Cleon here.

Plathane: O, if you meet him, call Hyperbolus!
    We'll pay you out today.

Hostess: O filthy throat,
    O how I'd like to take a stone and hack
    Those grinders out with which you chawed my wares.

Plathane: I'd like to pitch you in the deadman's pit.

Hostess: I'd like to get a reaping-hook and scoop
    That gullet out with which you gorged my tripe.
    But I'll to Cleon. He'll soon serve his writs;
    He'll twist it out of you today, he will....
    (Exeunt Hostess and Plathane.)
    (Re-enter Aeacus with assistants.)

Aeacus: Seize the dog-stealer, bind him, pinion him,
　　Drag him to justice.
Dionysus: Somebody's going to catch it.
Xanthias: *(striking out)* Hands off! Away! Stand back!
Aeacus: Eh? You're for fighting.
　　Ho! Ditylas, Sceblyas, and Pardocas,
　　Come hither, quick. Fight me this sturdy knave.
Dionysus: Now isn't it a shame the man should strike
　　And he a thief besides?
Aeacus: A monstrous shame!
Dionysus: A regular burning shame!
Xanthias: By the Lord Zeus,
　　If ever I was here before, if ever
　　I stole one hair's-worth from you, let me die!
　　And now I'll make you a right noble offer.
　　Arrest my lad. Torture him as you will,
　　And if you find I'm guilty, take and kill me.
Aeacus: Torture him, how?
Xanthias: In any mode you please.
　　Pile bricks upon him. Stuff his nose with acid.
　　Flay, rack him, hoist him. Flog him with a scourge
　　Of prickly bristles. Only not with this,
　　A soft-leaved onion or a tender leek.
Aeacus: A fair proposal. If I strike too hard
　　And maim the boy, I'll make you compensation.
Xanthias: I shan't require it. Take him out and flog him.
Aeacus: Nay, but I'll do it here before your eyes.
　　Now then, put down the traps, and mind you speak
　　The truth, young fellow.
Dionysus: *(in agony)* Man, don't torture me!
　　I am a god. You'll blame yourself hereafter
　　If you touch me.
Aeacus: Hillo! What's that you are saying?
Dionysus: I say I'm Bacchus, son of Zeus, a god,
　　And he's the slave.
Aeacus: You hear him?

Xanthias: Hear him? Yes.
    All the more reason you should flog him well.
    For if he is a god, he won't perceive it.
Dionysus: Well, but you say that you're a god yourself.
    So why not you be flogged as well as I?
Xanthias: A fair proposal. And be this the test,
    Whichever of us two you first behold
    Flinching or crying out, he's not the god.
Aeacus: Upon my word you're quite the gentleman.
    You're all for right and justice. Strip then, both.
Xanthias: How can you test us fairly?
Aeacus: Easily. I'll give you blow for blow.
Xanthias: A good idea.
    We're ready now!
    (Aeacus strikes him.) See if you catch me flinching.
Aeacus: I struck you.
Xanthias: *(incredulously)* No!
Aeacus: Well, it seems "no" indeed.
    Now then I'll strike the other.
    (strikes Dionysus)
Dionysus: Tell me when?
Aeacus: I struck you.
Dionysus: Struck me? Then why didn't I sneeze?
Aeacus: Don't know, I'm sure. I'll try the other again.
Xanthias: And quickly too. Good gracious!
Aeacus: Why "good gracious"?
    Not hurt you, did I?
Xanthias: No, I merely thought of
    The Diomeian feast of Heracles.
Aeacus: A holy man! 'Tis now the other's turn.
Dionysus: Hi! Hi!
Aeacus: Hallo!
Dionysus: Look at those horsemen, look!
Aeacus: But why these tears?
Dionysus: There's such a smell of onions.
Aeacus: Then you don't mind it?

Dionysus: (*cheerfully*) Mind it? Not a bit.
Aeacus: Well, I must go to the other one again.
Xanthias: O! O!
Aeacus: Hallo!
Xanthias: Do pray pull out this thorn.
Aeacus: What does it mean? 'Tis this one's turn again.
Dionysus: (*shrieking*) Apollo! Lord!
        (*calmly*) of Delos and of Pytho.
Xanthias: He flinched! You heard him?
Dionysus: Not at all! A jolly verse of Hipponax
        flashed across my mind.
Xanthias: You don't half do it. Cut his flanks to pieces.
Aeacus: By Zeus, well thought on. Turn
        your belly here.
Dionysus: (*screaming*) Poseidon!
Xanthias: There! He's flinching.
Dionysus: (*singing*) ...who dost reign
   Amongst the Aegean peaks and creeks
   And o'er the deep blue main.
Aeacus: No, by Demeter, still I can't find out
   Which is the god, but come you both indoors.
   My lord himself and Persephassa there,
   Being gods themselves, will soon find out the truth.
Dionysus: Right! Right! I only wish you had thought
        of that
   Before you gave me those tremendous whacks....
   (*Exeunt Dionysus, Xanthias, Aeacus, and attendants.*)

3. Cerberus, the three-headed dog who guards the gates of the underworld. Hellenistic painting, c. 3rd century BCE, Sidonian Burial Caves (southern Israel). (Photo, Ian Scott)

6. Orphic Lamina[6]

from Hipponium (Vibo Valentia)

Greek, 400 BCE

To Mnemosyne this text is sacred: (for Mystes) when you
would be on the point of dying.

You will go to the well-built houses of Hades. There is a
spring on the right.
Next to it there rises a white cypress.
There the souls of the dead descend to cool themselves.
Do not even approach this spring,
But further on you will find the cold water running
From the lake of Mnemosyne. There in front are the
guardians,
And they will demand of you, for sure understanding,
What do you seek across the shadows of foggy Hades.
Say: "I am the son of Earth and the Starry Sky.
I am dry of thirst, and I approach. But give me right away
The cold water coming from Lake Mnemosyne to drink."
And they, not merciful by the will of the ruler of the
underworld,
Will give you the water of Lake Mnemosyne to drink.
And when you have drunk, you will walk through the
sacred path on which also the other
Glorious initiates with their branches make their
procession.

4.   Aeacus, Rhadamanthus and Minos, underworld judges of the dead. Greek terracotta krater, c. 350 BCE, from Altamura, Apulia (southern Italy). National Archaeological Museum of Naples.

7. GORGIAS[7]

BY PLATO (428/427 OR 424/423 – 348/347 BCE)

Greek, c. 380 BCE

Socrates: Give ear then, as they say, to a right fine story, which you will regard as a fable, I fancy, but I as an actual account, for what I am about to tell you I mean to offer as the truth. By Homer's account, Zeus, Poseidon, and Pluto divided the sovereignty amongst them when they took it over from their father.

Now in the time of Cronos there was a law concerning mankind, and it holds to this very day amongst the gods, that every man who has passed a just and holy life departs after his decease to the Isles of the Blest and dwells in all happiness apart from ill, but whoever has lived unjustly and impiously goes to the dungeon of requital and penance which, you know, they call Tartarus.

Of these men there were judges in Cronos's time, and still of late in the reign of Zeus — living men to judge the living upon the day when each was to breathe his last. And thus the cases were being decided amiss. So Pluto and the overseers from the Isles of the Blest came before Zeus with the report that they found men passing over to either abode undeserving. Then spake Zeus: "Nay," said he, "I will put a stop to these proceedings. The cases are now indeed judged ill, and it is because they who are on trial are tried in their clothing, for they are tried alive. Now many," said he, "who have wicked souls are clad in fair bodies and ancestry and wealth, and at their judgment appear many witnesses to testify that their lives have been just.

Now, the judges are confounded not only by their evidence but at the same time by being clothed themselves while they sit in judgment, having their own soul muffled in the veil of eyes and ears and the whole body. Thus all these are a hindrance to them, their own habiliments no less than those of the judged. Well, first of all," he said, "we must put a stop to their foreknowledge of their death. For this they at present foreknow. However, Prometheus has already been given the word to stop this in them. Next they must be stripped bare of all those things before they are tried. For they must stand their trial dead.

Their judge also must be naked, dead, beholding with very soul the very soul of each immediately upon his death, bereft of all his kin and having left behind on earth all that fine array, to the end that the judgment may be just. Now I, knowing all this before you, have appointed sons of my own to be judges: two from Asia, Minos and Rhadamanthus, and one from Europe, Aeacus. These, when their life is ended, shall give judgment in the meadow at the dividing of the road, whence are the two ways leading, one to the Isles of the Blest and the other to Tartarus. And those who come from Asia shall Rhadamanthus try, and those from Europe, Aeacus. And to Minos I will give the privilege of the final decision, if the other two be in any doubt so that the judgment upon this journey of mankind may be supremely just."

"This, Callicles, is what I have heard and believe to be true. And from these stories, on my reckoning, we must draw some such moral as this: death, as it seems to me, is actually nothing but the disconnection of two things, the soul and the body, from each other. And so when they are disconnected from one another, each of them keeps its own condition very much as it was when the man was alive, the body having its own nature, with its treatments and experiences all manifest upon it.

For instance, if anyone's body was large by nature or by feeding or by both when he was alive, his corpse will be large also when he is dead. And if he was fat, it will be fat too after his death, and so on for the rest. Or again, if he used to follow the fashion of long hair, long-haired also will be his corpse. Again, if anyone had been a sturdy rogue and bore traces of his stripes in scars on his body, either from the whip or from other wounds, while yet alive, then after death too his body has these marks visible upon it. Or if anyone's limbs were broken or distorted in life, these same effects are manifest in death. In a word, whatever sort of bodily appearance a man had acquired in life, that is manifest also after his death either wholly or in the main for some time.

And so it seems to me that the same is the case with the soul too, Callicles. When a man's soul is stripped bare of the body, all its natural gifts and the experiences added to that soul as the result of his various pursuits are manifest in it. So when they have arrived in presence of their judge, they of Asia before Rhadamanthus, these Rhadamanthus sets before him and surveys the soul of each, not knowing whose it is. Nay, often when he has laid hold of the Great King or some other prince or potentate, he perceives the utter unhealthiness of his soul, striped all over with the scourge and a mass of wounds, the work of perjuries and injustice; where every act has left its smirch upon his soul, where all is awry through falsehood and imposture, and nothing straight because of a nurture that knew not truth: or, as the result of an unbridled course of fastidiousness, insolence, and incontinence, he finds the soul full fraught with disproportion and ugliness. Beholding this he sends it away in dishonor straight to the place of custody, where on its arrival it is to endure the sufferings that are fitting.

And it is fitting that every one under punishment rightly inflicted on him by another should either be made better and profit thereby or serve as an example to the rest, that others seeing the sufferings he endures may in fear amend themselves. Those who are benefited by the punishment they get from gods and men are they who have committed remediable offences. But still it is through bitter throes of pain that they receive their benefit both here and in the netherworld, for in no other way can there be riddance of iniquity. But of those who have done extreme wrong and, as a result of such crimes, have become incurable, of those are the examples made. No longer are they profited at all themselves, since they are incurable, but others are profited who behold them undergoing for their transgressions the greatest, sharpest, and most fearful sufferings evermore, actually hung up as examples there in the infernal dungeon, a spectacle and a lesson to such of the wrongdoers as arrive from time to time.

Among them I say Archelaus also will be found, if what Polus tells us is true, and every other despot of his sort. And I think, moreover, that most of these examples have come from despots and kings and potentates and public administrators, for these, since they have a free hand, commit the greatest and most impious offences.

Homer also testifies to this, for he has represented kings and potentates as those who are punished everlastingly in the netherworld — Tantalus and Sisyphus and Tityus. But Thersites, or any other private person who was wicked, has been portrayed by none as incurable and therefore subjected to heavy punishment, no doubt because he had not a free hand, and therefore was in fact happier than those who had. For in fact, Callicles, it is among the powerful that we find the specially wicked men. Still there is nothing to prevent good men being found even among these, and it deserves our special admiration when they are, for it is hard, Callicles, and deserving of no slight praise, when a man with a perfectly free hand for injustice lives always a just life. The men of this sort are but few, for indeed there have been, and I expect there yet will be, both here and elsewhere, men of honor and excellence in this virtue of administering justly what is committed to their charge.

One in fact there has been whose fame stands high among us and throughout the rest of Greece: Aristeides, son of Lysimachus. But most of those in power, my excellent friend, prove to be bad. So, as I was saying, whenever the judge Rhadamanthus has to deal with such a one, he knows nothing else of him at all, neither who he is nor of what descent, but only that he is a wicked person and on perceiving this he sends him away to Tartarus, first setting a mark on him to show whether he deems it a curable or an incurable case.

8. PHAEDO[8]

BY PLATO (428/427 OR 424/423 – 348/347 BCE)

Greek, c. 380 BCE

Socrates: One of the chasms of the earth is greater than the rest and is bored right through the whole earth. This is the one which Homer means when he says, "Far off, the lowest abyss beneath the earth," and which elsewhere he and many other poets have called Tartarus. For all the rivers flow together into this chasm and flow out of it again, and they have each the nature of the earth through which they flow. And the reason why all the streams flow in and out here is that this liquid matter has no bottom or foundation. So it oscillates and waves up and down, and the air and wind about it do the same, for they follow the liquid both when it moves toward the other side of the earth and when it moves toward this side, and just as the breath of those who breathe blows in and out, so the wind there oscillates with the liquid and causes terrible and irresistible blasts as it rushes in and out.

And when the water retires to the region that we call the lower, it flows into the rivers there and fills them up, as if it were pumped into them. And when it leaves that region and comes back to this side, it fills the rivers here. And when the streams are filled they flow through the passages and through the earth and come to the various places to which their different paths lead, where they make seas and marshes, and rivers and springs.

Thence they go down again under the earth, some passing around many great regions and others around fewer and smaller places, and flow again into Tartarus, some much below the point where they were sucked out, and some only a little. But all flow in below their exit. Some flow in on the side from which they flowed out, others on the opposite side. And some pass completely around in a circle, coiling about the earth once or several times, like serpents, then descend to the lowest possible depth and fall again into the chasm.

Now it is possible to go down from each side to the center, but not beyond, for there the slope rises forward in front of the streams from either side of the earth. Now these streams are many and great and of all sorts, but among the many are four streams, the greatest and outermost of which is that called Oceanus, which flows round in a circle, and opposite this, flowing in the opposite direction, is Acheron, which flows through various desert places and, passing under the earth, comes to the Acherusian Lake. To this lake the souls of most of the dead go and, after remaining there the appointed time, which is for some longer and for others shorter, are sent back to be born again into living beings.

The third river flows out between these two, and near the place whence it issues it falls into a vast region burning with a great fire and makes a lake larger than our Mediterranean Sea, boiling with water and mud. Thence it flows in a circle, turbid and muddy, and comes in its winding course, among other places, to the edge of the Acherusian Lake, but does not mingle with its water. Then, after winding about many times underground, it flows into Tartarus at a lower level. This is the river called Pyriphlegethon, and the streams of lava that spout up at various places on earth are offshoots from it.

Opposite this the fourth river issues, it is said, first into a wild and awful place, which is all of a dark blue color, like lapis lazuli. This is called the Stygian river, and the lake which it forms by flowing in is the Styx. And when the river has flowed in here and has received fearful powers into its waters, it passes under the earth and, circling round in the direction opposed to that of Pyriphlegethon, it meets it coming from the other way in the Acherusian Lake. And the water of this river also mingles with no other water, but this also passes round in a circle and falls into Tartarus opposite Pyriphlegethon. And the name of this river, as the poets say, is Cocytus. Such is the nature of these things.

Now when the dead have come to the place where each is led by his genius, first they are judged and sentenced, as they have lived well and piously, or not. And those who are found to have lived neither well nor ill, go to the Acheron and, embarking upon vessels provided for them, arrive in them at the lake. There they dwell and are purified, and if they have done any wrong they are absolved by paying the penalty for their wrong doings, and for their good deeds they receive rewards, each according to his merits.

But those who appear to be incurable, on account of the greatness of their wrongdoings, because they have committed many great deeds of sacrilege, or wicked and abominable murders, or any other such crimes, are cast by their fitting destiny into Tartarus, whence they never emerge.

Those, however, who are curable, but are found to have committed great sins — who have, for example, in a moment of passion done some act of violence against father or mother and have lived in repentance the rest of their lives, or who have slain some other person under similar conditions — these must needs be thrown into Tartarus, and when they have been there a year the wave casts them out, the homicides by way of Cocytus, those who have outraged their parents by way of Pyriphlegethon.

And when they have been brought by the current to the Acherusian Lake, they shout and cry out, calling to those whom they have slain or outraged, begging and beseeching them to be gracious and to let them come out into the lake. And if they prevail, they come out and cease from their ills, but if not, they are borne away again to Tartarus and thence back into the rivers, and this goes on until they prevail upon those whom they have wronged. This is the penalty imposed upon them by the judges.

But those who are found to have excelled in holy living are freed from these regions within the earth and are released as from prisons. They mount upward into their pure abode and dwell upon the earth. And of these, all who have duly purified themselves by philosophy live henceforth altogether without bodies and pass to still more beautiful abodes, which it is not easy to describe, nor have we now time enough.

9. THE REPUBLIC[9]

BY PLATO (428/427 OR 424/423 – 348/347 BCE)

Greek, c. 380 BCE

Socrates: It is not, let me tell you, the tale to Alcinous told
that I shall unfold, but the tale of a warrior bold, Er, the son
of Armenius, by race a Pamphylian. He once upon a time
was slain in battle, and when the corpses were taken up
on the tenth day already decayed, was found intact, and
having been brought home, at the moment of his funeral,
on the twelfth day as he lay upon the pyre, revived, and
after coming to life related what, he said, he had seen in
the world beyond.

He said that when his soul went forth from his body he
journeyed with a great company and that they came to a
mysterious region where there were two openings side by
side in the earth, and above and over against them in the
heaven two others, and that judges were sitting between
these, and that after every judgment they bade the righteous
journey to the right and upwards through the heaven with
tokens attached to them in front of the judgment passed
upon them, and the unjust to take the road to the left and
downward, they too wearing behind signs of all that had
befallen them, and that when he himself drew near they
told him that he must be the messenger to mankind to tell
them of that other world, and they charged him to give ear
and to observe everything in the place.

And so he said that here he saw, by each opening of
heaven and earth, the souls departing after judgment
had been passed upon them, while, by the other pair of
openings, there came up from the one in the earth souls
full of squalor and dust, and from the second there came
down from heaven a second procession of souls clean
and pure, and that those who arrived from time to time

appeared to have come as it were from a long journey and gladly departed to the meadow and encamped there as at a festival, and acquaintances greeted one another, and those who came from the earth questioned the others about conditions up yonder, and those from heaven asked how it fared with those others.

And they told their stories to one another, the one lamenting and wailing as they recalled how many and how dreadful things they had suffered and seen in their journey beneath the earth — it lasted a thousand years — while those from heaven related their delights and visions of a beauty beyond words.

To tell it all, Glaucon, would take all our time, but the sum, he said, was this. For all the wrongs they had ever done to anyone and all whom they had severally wronged, they had paid the penalty in turn tenfold for each, and the measure of this was by periods of a hundred years each, so that on the assumption that this was the length of human life the punishment might be ten times the crime. For example, if anyone had been the cause of many deaths or had betrayed cities and armies and reduced them to slavery, or had been participant in any other iniquity, they might receive in requital pains tenfold for each of these wrongs. And again if any had done deeds of kindness and been just and holy men they might receive their due reward in the same measure; and other things not worthy of record he said of those who had just been born and lived but a short time; and he had still greater requitals to tell of piety and impiety towards the gods and parents and of self-slaughter.

For he said that he stood by when one was questioned by another: "Where is Ardiaeos the Great?" Now this Ardiaeos had been tyrant in a certain city of Pamphylia just a thousand years before that time and had put to death his old father and his elder brother and had done many other unholy deeds, as was the report. So he said that the one questioned replied, "He has not come," said he, "nor will he be likely to come here. For indeed this was one of the dreadful sights we beheld. When we were near the mouth and about to issue forth and all our other sufferings were ended, we suddenly caught sight of him and of others, the most of them, I may say, tyrants. But there were some of private station, of those who had committed great crimes. And when these supposed that at last they were about to go up and out, the mouth would not receive them, but it bellowed when anyone of the incurably wicked or of those who had not completed their punishment tried to come up."

And thereupon, he said, savage men of fiery aspect who stood by and took note of the voice laid hold on them and bore them away. But Ardiaeos and others they bound hand and foot and head and flung down and flayed them and dragged them by the wayside, carding them on thorns and signifying to those who from time to time passed by for what cause they were borne away, and that they were to be hurled into Tartarus.

And then, though many and manifold dread things had befallen them, this fear exceeded all — lest each one should hear the voice when he tried to go up, and each went up most gladly when it had kept silence. And the judgments and penalties were somewhat after this manner, and the blessings were their counterparts.

5.   Harpy with a shade. Greek tomb relief, c. 480–70 BCE,
Lycia, found at Xanthus, Anatolia (western Turkey). British
Museum. (Photo, Carole Raddato)

10. THE AENEID[10]

BY VIRGIL (70–19 BCE)

Roman, 19 BCE

Book 6
After these toils, they [Aeneas and the Sibyl] hasten
    to fulfil
What else the Sibyl said. Straightway they find
A cave profound, of entrance gaping wide,
O'erhung with rock, in gloom of sheltering grove,
Near the dark waters of a lake, whereby
No bird might ever pass with scathless wing,
So dire an exhalation is breathed out
From that dark deep of death to upper air.
Hence, in the Grecian tongue, Aornos called.
Here first four youthful bulls of swarthy hide
Were led for sacrifice. On each broad brow
The priestess sprinkled wine; 'twixt the two horns
Outplucked the lifted hair, and cast it forth
Upon the holy flames, beginning so
Her offerings; then loudly sued the power
of Hecate, a queen in heaven and hell.
Some struck with knives and caught in shallow bowls
The smoking blood. Aeneas's lifted hand
Smote with a sword a sable-fleeced ewe
To Night, the mother of th' Eumenides,
And Earth, her sister dread; next unto thee,
O Proserpine, a curst and barren cow;
Then unto Pluto, Stygian king, he built
An altar dark, and piled upon the flames
The ponderous entrails of the bulls and poured
Free o'er the burning flesh the goodly oil.
Then lo! at dawn's dim, earliest beam began
Beneath their feet a groaning of the ground.

The wooded hill-tops shook, and, as it seemed,
She-hounds of hell howled viewless through the
    shade
To hail their queen. "Away, O souls profane!
Stand far away!" the priestess shrieked, "Nor dare
Unto this grove come near! Aeneas, on!
Begin thy journey! Draw thy sheathed blade!
Now, all thy courage! Now, th'unshaken soul!"
She spoke and burst into the yawning cave
With frenzied step. He follows where she leads
And strides with feet unfaltering at her side.
Ye gods, who rule the spirits of the dead!
Ye voiceless shades and silent lands of night!
O Phlegethon! O Chaos! Let my song,
If it be lawful, in fit words declare
What I have heard and by your help divine
Unfold what hidden things enshrouded lie
In that dark underworld of sightless gloom.
They walked exploring the unpeopled night
Through Pluto's vacuous realms and regions void,
As when one's path in dreary woodlands winds
Beneath a misty moon's deceiving ray,
When Jove has mantled all his heaven in shade,
And night seals up the beauty of the world.
In the first courts and entrances of hell
Sorrows and vengeful Cares on couches lie:
There sad Old Age abides, Diseases pale,
And Fear, and Hunger, temptress to all crime;
Want, base and vile, and, two dread shapes to see,
Bondage and Death: then Sleep, Death's next of kin;
And dreams of guilty joy. Death-dealing War
Is ever at the doors, and hard thereby
The Furies' beds of steel, where wild-eyed Strife
Her snaky hair with blood-stained fillet binds.
There in the middle court a shadowy elm
Its ancient branches spreads, and in its leaves

Deluding visions ever haunt and cling.
Then come strange prodigies of bestial kind:
Centaurs are stabled there, and double shapes
Like Scylla, or the dragon Lerna bred,
With hideous scream; Briareos clutching far
His hundred hands, Chimera girt with flame,
A crowd of Gorgons, Harpies of foul wing,
And giant Geryon's triple-monstered shade.
Aeneas, shuddering with sudden fear,
Drew sword and fronted them with naked steel;
And, save his sage conductress bade him know
These were but shapes and shadows sweeping by,
His stroke had cloven in vain the vacant air.
Hence the way leads to that Tartarean stream
Of Acheron, whose torrent fierce and foul
Disgorges in Cocytus all its sands.
A ferryman of gruesome guise keeps ward
Upon these waters — Charon, foully garbed,
With unkempt, thick gray beard upon his chin,
And staring eyes of flame; a mantle coarse,
All stained and knotted, from his shoulder falls,
As with a pole he guides his craft, tends sail,
And in the black boat ferries o'er his dead.
Old, but a god's old age looks fresh and strong.
To those dim shores the multitude streams on —
Husbands and wives, and pale, unbreathing forms
Of high-souled heroes, boys and virgins fair,
And strong youth at whose graves fond parents
        mourned.
As numberless the throng as leaves that fall
When autumn's early frost is on the grove,
Or like vast flocks of birds by winter's chill
Sent flying o'er wide seas to lands of flowers.
All stood beseeching to begin their voyage
Across that river and reached out pale hands
In passionate yearning for its distant shore.

But the grim boatman takes now these, now those,
Or thrusts unpitying from the stream away.
Aeneas, moved to wonder and deep awe,
Beheld the tumult. "Virgin seer!" he cried,
"Why move the thronging ghosts toward yonder
       stream?
What seek they there? Or what election holds
That these unwilling linger, while their peers
Sweep forward yonder o'er the leaden waves?"
To him, in few, the aged Sibyl spoke:
"Son of Anchises, offspring of the gods,
Yon are Cocytus and the Stygian stream,
By whose dread power the gods themselves do fear
To take an oath in vain. Here far and wide
Thou seest the hapless throng that hath no grave.
That boatman Charon bears across the deep
Such as be sepulchred with holy care.
But over that loud flood and dreadful shore
No trav'ler may be borne until in peace
His gathered ashes rest. A hundred years
Round this dark borderland some haunt and roam,
Then win late passage o'er the longed-for wave."
Aeneas lingered for a little space,
Revolving in his soul with pitying prayer
Fate's partial way....

The twain continue now their destined way
Unto the river's edge. The ferryman,
Who watched them through still groves approach
      his shore,
Hailed them, at distance, from the Stygian wave,
And with reproachful summons thus began:
"Whoe'er thou art that in this warrior guise
Unto my river comest, quickly tell
Thine errand! Stay thee where thou standest now!
This is ghosts' land, for sleep and slumbrous dark.

That flesh and blood my Stygian ship should bear
Were lawless wrong. Unwillingly I took
Alcides, Theseus, and Pirithous,
Though sons of gods, too mighty to be quelled.
One bound in chains yon warder of Hell's door
And dragged him trembling from our monarch's
        throne.
The others, impious, would steal away
Out of her bride-bed Pluto's ravished queen."
Briefly th' Amphrysian priestess made reply:
"Not ours, such guile. Fear not! This warrior's arms
Are innocent. Let Cerberus from his cave
Bay ceaselessly, the bloodless shades to scare.
Let Proserpine immaculately keep
The house and honor of her kinsman king.
Trojan Aeneas, famed for faithful prayer
And victory in arms, descends to seek
His father in this gloomy deep of death.
If loyal goodness move not such as thee,
This branch [the Golden Bough] at least (she drew it
        from her breast)
Thou knowest well."
Then cooled his wrathful heart.
With silent lips he looked and wondering eyes
Upon that fateful, venerable wand,
Seen only once an age. Shoreward he turned,
And pushed their way his boat of leaden hue.
The rows of crouching ghosts along the thwarts
He scattered, cleared a passage, and gave room
To great Aeneas. The light shallop groaned
Beneath his weight, and, straining at each seam,
Took in the foul flood with unstinted flow.
At last the hero and his priestess-guide
Came safe across the river and were moored
'Mid sea-green sedges in the formless mire.
Here Cerberus, with triple-throated roar,

Made all the region ring, as there he lay
At vast length in his cave. The Sibyl then,
Seeing the serpents writhe around his neck,
Threw down a loaf with honeyed herbs imbued
And drowsy essences. He, ravenous,
Gaped wide his three fierce mouths and snatched the bait,
Crouched with his large backs loose upon the ground
And filled his cavern floor from end to end.
Aeneas through hell's portal moved, while sleep
Its warder buried. Then he fled that shore
Of Stygian stream, whence travellers ne'er return.
Now hears he sobs and piteous, lisping cries
Of souls of babes upon the threshold plaining,
Whom, ere they took their portion of sweet life,
Dark Fate from nursing bosoms tore, and plunged
In bitterness of death. Nor far from these,
The throng of dead by unjust judgment slain.
Not without judge or law these realms abide:
Wise Minos there the urn of justice moves
And holds assembly of the silent shades,
Hearing the stories of their lives and deeds.
Close on this place those doleful ghosts abide,
Who, not for crime, but loathing life and light
With their own hands took death and cast away
The vital essence. Willingly, alas!
They now would suffer need or burdens bear,
If only life were given! But Fate forbids.
Around them winds the sad, unlovely wave
Of Styx. Nine times it coils and interflows.
Not far from hence, on every side outspread,
The Fields of Sorrow lie — such name they bear.
Here all whom ruthless love did waste away
Wander in paths unseen or in the gloom
Of a dark myrtle grove. Not even in death
Have they forgot their griefs of long ago.
Here impious Phaedra and poor Procris bide.

Lorn Eriphyle bares the vengeful wounds
Her own son's dagger made. Evadne here,
And foul Pasiphaë are seen, hard by,
Laodamia, nobly fond and fair,
And Caeneus, not a boy, but maiden now,
By Fate remoulded to her native seeming.
Here Tyrian Dido, too, her wound unhealed,
Roamed through a mighty wood. The Trojan's eyes
Beheld her near him through the murky gloom,
As when, in her young month and crescent pale,
One sees th' o'er-clouded moon, or thinks he sees.
Down dropped his tears, and thus he fondly spoke:
"O suffering Dido! Were those tidings true
That thou didst fling thee on the fatal steel?
Thy death, ah me! I dealt it. But I swear
By stars above us, by the powers in heaven,
Or whatsoever oath ye dead believe,
That not by choice I fled thy shores, O Queen!
Divine decrees compelled me, even as now
Among these ghosts I pass and thread my way
Along this gulf of night and loathsome land.
How could I deem my cruel taking leave
Would bring thee at the last to all this woe?
O, stay! Why shun me? Wherefore haste away?
Our last farewell! Our doom! I speak it now!"
Thus, though she glared with fierce, relentless gaze,
Aeneas, with fond words and tearful plea
Would soothe her angry soul. But on the ground
She fixed averted eyes. For all he spoke
Moved her no more than if her frowning brow
Were changeless flint or carved in Parian stone.
Then, after pause, away in wrath she fled
And refuge took within the cool, dark grove,
Where her first spouse, Sichaeus, with her tears
Mingled his own in mutual love and true.
Aeneas, none the less, her guiltless woe

With anguish knew, watched with dimmed eyes her way
And pitied from afar the fallen queen.
Aeneas straightway by the leftward cliff
Beheld a spreading rampart, high begirt
With triple wall, and circling round it ran
A raging river of swift floods of flame,
Infernal Phlegethon, which whirls along
Loud-thundering rocks. A mighty gate is there
Columned in adamant. No human power,
Nor even the gods, against this gate prevail.
Tall tower of steel it has, and seated there
Tisiphone, in blood-flecked pall arrayed,
Sleepless forever, guards the entering way.
Hence groans are heard, fierce cracks of lash and scourge,
Loud-clanking iron links and trailing chains.
Aeneas motionless with horror stood
O'erwhelmed at such uproar. "O virgin, say
What shapes of guilt are these? What penal woe
Harries them thus? What wailing smites the air?"
To whom the Sibyl, "Far-famed prince of Troy,
The feet of innocence may never pass
Into this house of sin. But Hecate,
When o'er th' Avernian groves she gave me power,
Taught me what penalties the gods decree,
And showed me all. There Cretan Rhadamanth
His kingdom keeps and from unpitying throne
Chastises and lays bare the secret sins
Of mortals who, exulting in vain guile,
Elude till death their expiation due.
There, armed forever with her vengeful scourge,
Tisiphone, with menace and affront,
The guilty swarm pursues. In her left hand
She lifts her angered serpents, while she calls
A troop of sister-furies fierce as she.
Then, grating loud on hinge of sickening sound,
Hell's portals open wide. O, dost thou see

What sentinel upon that threshold sits?
What shapes of fear keep guard upon that gloom?
Far, far within the dragon Hydra broods
With half a hundred mouths gaping and black.
And Tartarus slopes downward to the dark
Twice the whole space that in the realms of light
Th' Olympian heaven above our earth aspires.
Here Earth's first offspring, the Titanic brood,
Roll lightning-blasted in the gulf profound.
The twin Aloïdae, colossal shades,
Came on my view. Their hands made stroke at heaven
And strove to thrust Jove from his seat on high.
I saw Salmoneus his dread stripes endure,
Who dared to counterfeit Olympian thunder
And Jove's own fire. In chariot of four steeds,
Brandishing torches, he triumphant rode
Through throngs of Greeks, o'er Elis's sacred way,
Demanding worship as a god. O fool!
To mock the storm's inimitable flash
With crash of hoofs and roll of brazen wheel!
But mightiest Jove from rampart of thick cloud
Hurled his own shaft, no flickering, mortal flame,
And in vast whirl of tempest laid him low.
Next unto these, on Tityus I looked,
Child of old Earth, whose womb all creatures bears.
Stretched o'er nine roods he lies. A vulture huge
Tears with hooked beak at his immortal side
Or deep in entrails ever rife with pain
Gropes for a feast, making his haunt and home
In the great Titan bosom, nor will give
To ever new-born flesh surcease of woe.
Why name Ixion and Pirithous,
The Lapithae, above whose impious brows
A crag of flint hangs quaking to its fall,
As if just toppling down, while couches proud,
Propped upon golden pillars, bid them feast

In royal glory. But beside them lies
The eldest of the Furies, whose dread hands
Thrust from the feast away and wave aloft
A flashing firebrand with shrieks of woe.
Here in a prison-house awaiting doom
Are men who hated, long as life endured,
Their brothers, or maltreated their gray sires,
Or tricked a humble friend; the men who grasped
At hoarded riches, with their kith and kin
Not sharing ever — an unnumbered throng;
Here slain adulterers be; and men who dared
To fight in unjust cause and break all faith
With their own lawful lords. Seek not to know
What forms of woe they feel, what fateful shape
Of retribution hath o'erwhelmed them there.
Some roll huge boulders up. Some hang on wheels
Lashed to the whirling spokes. In his sad seat
Theseus is sitting, nevermore to rise.
Unhappy Phlegyas uplifts his voice
In warning through the darkness, calling loud,
'O, ere too late, learn justice and fear God!'
Yon traitor sold his country, and for gold
Enchained her to a tyrant, trafficking
In laws, for bribes enacted or made void.
Another did incestuously assail
His daughter's bed with infamous embrace.
All ventured some unclean, prodigious crime,
And what they dared, achieved. I could not tell,
Not with a hundred mouths, a hundred tongues,
Or iron voice, their divers shapes of sin,
Nor call by name the myriad pangs they bear."...

After these things Aeneas was aware
Of solemn groves in one deep, distant vale,
Where trees were whispering, and forever flowed
The river Lethe, through its land of calm.

Nations unnumbered roved and haunted there:
As when, upon a windless summer morn,
The bees afield among the rainbow flowers
Alight and sip, or round the lilies pure
Pour forth in busy swarm, while far diffused
Their murmured songs from all the meadows rise.
Aeneas in amaze the wonder views,
And fearfully inquires of whence and why;
What yonder rivers be; what people press,
Line after line, on those dim shores along.
Said Sire Anchises: "Yonder thronging souls
To reincarnate shape predestined move.
Here, at the river Lethe's wave, they quaff
Care-quelling floods, and long oblivion.
Of these I shall discourse, and to thy soul
Make visible the number and array
Of my posterity; so shall thy heart
In Italy, thy new-found home, rejoice."
"O father," said Aeneas, "must I deem
That from this region souls exalted rise
To upper air, and shall once more return
To cumbering flesh? O, wherefore do they feel,
Unhappy ones, such fatal lust to live?"
"I speak, my son, nor make thee longer doubt,"
Anchises said, and thus the truth set forth,
In ordered words from point to point unfolding:
"Know first that heaven and earth and ocean's plain,
The moon's bright orb, and stars of Titan birth
Are nourished by one Life; one primal Mind,
Immingled with the vast and general frame,
Fills every part and stirs the mighty whole.
Thence man and beast, thence creatures of the air,
And all the swarming monsters that be found
Beneath the level of the marbled sea;
A fiery virtue, a celestial power,
Their native seeds retain; but bodies vile,

With limbs of clay and members born to die,
Encumber and o'ercloud; whence also spring
Terrors and passions, suffering and joy;
For from deep darkness and captivity
All gaze but blindly on the radiant world.
Nor when to life's last beam they bid farewell
May sufferers cease from pain, nor quite be freed
From all their fleshly plagues, but by fixed law,
The strange, inveterate taint works deeply in.
For this, the chastisement of evils past
Is suffered here, and full requital paid.
Some hang on high, outstretched to viewless winds.
For some their sin's contagion must be purged
In vast ablution of deep-rolling seas
Or burned away in fire. Each man receives
His ghostly portion in the world of dark,
But thence to realms Elysian we go free,
Where for a few these seats of bliss abide,
Till time's long lapse a perfect orb fulfils,
And takes all taint away, restoring so
The pure, ethereal soul's first virgin fire.
At last, when the millennial aeon strikes,
God calls them forth to yon Lethaean stream,
In numerous host, that thence, oblivious all,
They may behold once more the vaulted sky
And willingly to shapes of flesh return."

11. METAMORPHOSES[11]

BY OVID (43 BCE–7 CE)

Roman, c. 8 CE

…While through the grass delighted Naiads wandered with Eurydice, the bride, a serpent struck its venomed tooth in her soft ankle — and she died.

After Orpheus, the bard of Rhodope, had mourned and filled the highs of heaven with the moans of his lament, determined also the dark underworld should recognize the misery of death, he dared descend by the Taenarian gate down to the gloomy Styx. And there passed through pale-glimmering phantoms and the ghosts escaped from sepulchres, until he found Persephone and Pluto, master-king of shadow realms below.

Then began to strike his tuneful lyre, to which he sang: "O deities of this dark world beneath the earth, this shadowy underworld, to which all mortals must descend, if it can be called lawful, and if you will suffer speech of strict truth — all the winding ways of Falsity forbidden — I come not down here because of curiosity to see the glooms of Tartarus and have no thought to bind or strangle the three necks of the Medusan Monster, vile with snakes. But I have come, because my darling wife stepped on a viper that sent through her veins death-poison, cutting off her coming years. If able, I would bear it, I do not deny my effort — but the god of Love has conquered me — a god so kindly known in all the upper world. We are not sure he can be known so well in this deep world but have good reason to conjecture he is not unknown here, and if old report almost forgotten, that you stole your wife is not a fiction, Love united you the same as others. By this Place of Fear this huge void and these vast and silent realms, renew the life-thread of Eurydice. All things are due to you, and though on earth it happens we may tarry a short while, slowly or swiftly we must go to one abode, and it will be our final home. Long and tenaciously you will possess unquestioned mastery of the human race. She also shall be yours to rule, when full of age she shall have lived the days of her allotted years. So I ask of you possession of her few days as a boon. But if the fates deny to me this prayer for my true wife, my constant mind must hold me always so that I cannot return— and you may triumph in the death of two!"

While he sang all his heart said to the sound of his sweet lyre, the bloodless ghosts themselves were weeping, and the anxious Tantalus stopped clutching at return-flow of the wave, Ixion's twisting wheel stood wonder-bound, and Tityus's liver for a while escaped the vultures, and the listening Belides forgot their sieve-like bowls and even you, O Sisyphus! sat idly on your rock!

Then Fame declared that conquered by the song of Orpheus, for the first and only time the hard cheeks of the fierce Eumenides were wet with tears, nor could the royal queen, nor he who rules the lower world deny the prayer of Orpheus. So they called to them Eurydice, who still was held among the new-arriving shades, and she obeyed the call by walking to them with slow steps, yet halting from her wound.

So Orpheus then received his wife, and Pluto told him he might now ascend from these Avernian vales up to the light with his Eurydice, but, if he turned his eyes to look at her, the gift of her delivery would be lost.

They picked their way in silence up a steep and gloomy path of darkness. There remained but little more to climb till they would touch earth's surface, when in fear he might again lose her and anxious for another look at her, he turned his eyes so he could gaze upon her.

Instantly she slipped away. He stretched out to her his despairing arms, eager to rescue her or feel her form but could hold nothing save the yielding air.

Dying the second time, she could not say a word of censure of her husband's fault. What had she to complain of — his great love? Her last word spoken was, "Farewell!" which he could barely hear, and with no further sound she fell from him again to Hades.

6.   Hermes, conductor of dead souls to the underworld, with Eurydice and Orpheus. Marble relief, copy of a Greek original of c. 450 BCE, from Torre del Greco (Naples). National Archaeological Museum of Naples. (Photo, Sailko)

12. MAD HERCULES[12]

BY SENECA (c. 4 BCE–65 CE)

Roman, after 81 CE

Cast of Characters (partial)

Hercules, son of Jupiter and Alcmena,
reputed son of Amphitryon
Amphitryon, husband of Alcmena
Theseus, king of Athens and friend of Hercules

Theseus: O god of heaven, and you who holdest sway
   In that deep, all-embracing realm of death,
   And you whose mother sought you, but in vain
   Through all the world: your powers I supplicate
   That I may speak with boldness of the things
   Concealed and buried in the hold of earth.
   The Spartan land lifts high a famous cliff
   Where Taenarus juts out upon the sea,
   Dense wooded. Here the realm of hated Dis
   Opes wide its mouth. The high cliff spreads apart,
   And in a mighty cavern yawns a pit
   With jaws portentous, huge, precipitous,
   And for all nations ample passage gives.
   The way begins, not dark with heavy shades.
   A watery gleam of daylight follows in,
   And doubtful light, as of the sun eclipsed,
   Falls there and mocks the eye. Such light the day,
   While mingled still with night, at early dawn
   Or in its waning hour, is wont to give.
   The way then broadens into spaces vast
   And empty, where the human race entire
   Might plunge and perish. 'Tis no labor here
   To travel, for the road itself draws down.
   As often whirlpools suck unwilling ships,

So does the air, down streaming, urge us on,
And hungry chaos. Here the clutching shades
Permit no backward step. Deep in the abyss,
With peaceful shallows gentle Lethe glides,
And by its draughts removes all mortal care
And, that no backward way may be allowed,
With many folds it wraps the stream of death,
Just as the wandering Maeander sports
With waves uncertain, now upon itself
Retreats, now halts in hesitation slow,
Whether it shall its fountain seek again,
Or journey to the sea. Here lies the marsh
Of sluggish, vile Cocytus. Here, behold
The vulture, there the doleful owl laments,
And through the air die fearsome screech-owl sends
Its sad, foreboding cry. There stands the yew,
Its black leaves shuddering on the gloomy boughs,
And 'neath its shelter hover sluggish Sleep,
And mournful Famine with her wasting jaws,
And Shame, at last her guilty face concealed.
Here quaking Fear and Murder, desperate Grief,
Black Mourning, tottering Disease, and War
With weapons girded on, lie hid. And last
Comes feeble Age upon his staff upheld.
Amphitryon: Are there no fruitful fields of corn or wine?
Theseus: Not so. No joyful fields with verdure shine,
No ripening grain waves gently in the breeze,
No stately trees bear apple-laden boughs;
But sterile wastes defile those lonely depths,
And in eternal sloth the foul earth lies.
Here lie the lonesome remnants of the world.
The air hangs motionless, and thick night broods
Upon a sluggish, horror-stricken land.
The place of death is worse than death itself.

Amphitryon: And what of him who rules those dusky realms?
    Where sits he as he rules his shadowy folk?
Theseus: There is a place in an obscure recess
    Of Tartarus, which, with its heavy shades,
    Dense vapor shrouds. Hence, from a single source,
    Two different rivers flow. With silent stream
    One bears along the sacred Stygian waves
    On which the gods take oath. With mighty roar
    The other fiercely rolls the rocks along
    Within its flood, the raging Acheron,
    Which may not be recrossed. Set opposite,
    By these two streams encircled, stands the hall
    Of royal Dis, and by a shading grove
    The mighty house is hid. A spacious cave
    Of overhanging rock the threshold forms.
    This is the path of souls. Here is the door
    Of Pluto's realm. And round about, there spreads
    The plain wherein the frowning monarch sits
    And new-come souls reviews. Of lowering brow
    And awful majesty the god appears.
    Yet in his face his brother's likeness bears
    And proves his noble birth. Jove's face is his,
    But thundering Jove's. And of that savage realm
    The master's self makes up the largest part,
    For every fearful thing holds him in fear.
Amphitryon: And is the story true that down below
    Stern justice is at last administered
    And guilty souls, who have their crimes forgot,
    At last atone for sin? Who is he, then,
    Who searches out the truth, and justice gives?
Theseus: There is not one inquisitor alone
    Who sits in judgment on the lofty seat
    And tries the trembling culprits. In that hall
    Sit Cretan Minos, Rhadamanthus too,
    And Aeacus. Each for his sins of earth
    Must suffer here. The crime returns to him

Who did it, and the guilty soul is crushed
By its own precedents. There, deep immured
In prison, bloody leaders have I seen,
And bleeding backs of heartless tyrants, scourged
By base plebeian hands. Who mildly reigns
And, though the lord of life, restrains his hands,
Who mercifully rules a bloodless realm
And spares the lives of men, he shall enjoy
Long years of happy life and at the end
Attain to heaven or to those regions blest
Of the Elysian Fields, himself a judge.
Refrain from human blood, all ye who rule.
Your sins with heavier judgment shall be judged.
Amphitryon: Does any certain place inclose the lost,
      And do, as rumor says, the impious
      Sharp punishments in endless chains endure?
Theseus: On swiftly flying wheel Ixion turns.
      And on the neck of Sisyphus a stone
      Weighs heavily. There stands in middle stream
      With throat thirst-parched, the poor old man and seeks
      To catch the cooling waves that wash his chin.
      He, oft deceived, hopes now at last to drink,
      As often fails the water at his lips.
      So also do the fruits his hunger fail.
      There Tityos eternal banquets gives
      Unto the greedy vulture, and in vain
      Do Danaus's daughters bear their brimming urns.
      There wander, raging still, the Cadmeids,
      And greedy birds still fright old Phineus.
Amphitryon: Now tell the noble struggle of my son.
      Does he bring back his uncle's willing gift,
      Or does he lead the dog as spoil of war?
Theseus: A gloomy cliff o'erhangs the sluggish shoals,
      Whose waves are dead and waters motionless.
      This stream is guarded by a grim old man,
      Of squalid garb and aspect hideous,

Who carries o'er the pool the quaking shades.
His long beard hangs unkempt. His shapeless robe
Is knotted into place. His fierce eyes gleam
From sunken cheeks. And he, as ferryman,
With his long pole propels his bark across.
He now his empty boat unto the shore
Was turning to receive the waiting souls,
When Hercules requested to be borne
Across the stream. The throng of shades give way.
But fiercely Charon cries: "Whither so bold
Do you hurry on? Stay there thy hurrying steps."
Alcmena's son would no delay endure,
But with the pole itself the boatman tamed,
And climbed aboard the boat. The roomy craft,
For nations ample, groaned beneath his weight.
And as he sat, the heavy-weighted skiff
With rocking sides drank in the Lethe stream.
Then quaked the conquered monsters at the sight:
The Centaurs, fierce and wild, the Lapithae,
Inflamed to strife by copious draughts of wine.
And, seeking out the farthest pools of Styx,
The beast of Lerna hid his fertile heads.
Soon there appeared the home of greedy Dis,
Where the fierce Stygian dog affrights the shades,
Who, tossing back and forth his triple heads,
With mighty bayings watches o'er the realm.
Around his head with damp corruption foul,
Writhe deadly serpents, and his shaggy mane
With vipers bristles, while a twisting snake
Forms his long, hissing tail. His wrath and form
Are both alike terrific. When he heard
The sound of coming feet, straightway he raised
His hackles, bristling with their darting snakes,
And with erected ears caught at the sound,
For even noiseless spirits can he hear.
When Jove's son nearer came, within his cave

The dog stood hesitant, and nameless fear
Each of the other felt. Then suddenly
The silence shudders with his bayings deep,
And threatening snakes along his shoulders hiss.
The clamor of his dreadful voice, sent forth
Three-throated, even happy shades dismayed.
Then did the hero from his left arm loose
The lion's skin with head and grinning jaws,
And 'neath this mighty shield opposed the dog.
Then in his right all conquering, he raised
His mighty club, and with a rain of blows,
Now here, now there, he drove the frightened beast.
The conquered dog at last gave o'er his threats
And, spent with fighting, lowered all his heads
And left the entrance free. Then did the king
And queen of hell sit trembling on their thrones
And bade the dog be led away. Me, too,
Did Dis at Hercules' request release,
A royal gift. Then with his soothing hand
Hercules stroked the monster's massive necks,
And bound him with an adamantine chain.
The watchful guardian of the dusky world
Forgot his wonted fierceness, and his ears
Drooped timidly. He let himself be led,
Confessed his master, and, with muzzle low,
Submissively he went, his snaky tail
Beating his sides the while. But when he came
To Taenarus, and in his eyes there smote
The gleam of unknown light, though strongly bound,
His courage he regained and madly shook
His mighty chains. Even his conqueror
Was backward borne and forced to yield his stand.
Then even my aid did the hero seek,
And with united strength we dragged the dog,
Still mad with rage, attempting fruitless war,
Into the upper world. But when he saw

The gleaming spaces of the shining sky,
The light of day, thick darkness blinded him.
He turned his gaze to earth and closed his eyes,
Expelled the hated light, looked backward, sought
With all his necks the sheltering earth, and last,
He hid his head within Hercules' shade.
But see, a mighty throng with shouts of joy
Comes yonder, wearing laurel on their brows,
Who chant the well-earned praise of Hercules.
Chorus: Eurystheus, brought untimely forth,
    Had bidden Hercules to pierce
    The depths of earth. This task alone
    Of all his labors yet remained —
    To rob the dusky king of hell.
    He dared to enter that dark way,
    Which to the distant manes leads,
    Dismal, with gloomy forests set,
    Yet crowded with the thronging souls.
    As when the eager people haste
    Throughout the city to behold
    The play in some new theater;
    As when they crowd the Pisan fields
    When the fifth summer brings again
    The Elean Thunderer's sacred games;
    As, when the lengthening nights return,
    And the balanced Scales the sun's bright car
    Detain, to gentle sleep inclined,
    The people throng the mysteries
    Of Ceres, while the Attic priests
    Lead through the fields with hurried steps
    The worshipers. Such thronging hordes
    Are driven through those silent plains.
    A part goes slow with steps of age,
    Sadly, and sated with the years.
    Some, in the earlier flush of life,
    Advance with the sprightly step of youth,

Young maids not yet in wedlock joined,
And boys with flowing ringlets, babes,
Who have not yet learned to repeat
Their mother's name. To these alone
'Tis given to dispel the night
With torches, and their fears relieve.
The rest in utter darkness fare
And sadness. So our spirits mourn,
When each one, grieving o'er his fate,
Feels crushed in darkness 'neath the weight
Of all the world. There chaos reigns,
Repulsive glooms, the hateful dark
Of night, the empty veil of clouds,
The weary inactivity
Of that still, empty universe.
Oh, may the time far distant be
When old age bears us to that land.
None come too late, and ne'er can he,
Who once has come, return again.
What need to hasten cruel fate?
For all the wandering tribes of earth
Shall surely seek the land of shades,
And on the still Cocytus spread
Their sails. All things the sun beholds,
In rising and in setting, grow
But to decay. Then spare, O death,
Those who are doomed to come to thee.
Life is but practicing for death.
Though you be slow in coming, still
We hasten of ourselves. The hour
That gave us life begins our death.
The joyful day of Thebes is here.
Now at the altars sacrifice
And let the choicest victims fall.
You maids and men, in mingled bands
Begin the stately choral dance,

And let the cattle of the fields
Put off their yokes and be glad today,
For by the hand of Hercules
Has peace from east to west been won
And in that land where the sun rides high
In middle heaven and the shadows fail.
Whatever region Tethys laves
In her long reach has been o'ercome
By great Hercules' toils. Borne now
Across the shoals of Tartarus,
With hell subdued, he comes again.
No room is left for fear. For what
Beyond the world of death remains?

7. Charon ferrying across the Styx. Tomb painting, 4th century BCE, Lucania (southern Italy). National Archaeological Museum of Paestum.

13. Vision of Thespesius[13]

by Plutarch (45?–120? ce)

Greek, after 81 ce

I came to tell them about a certain relative and friend of Protogenes, whom they knew because he had once visited us here. This man, a native of Soli, had denied himself no sensual indulgence in his youth. Then, having swiftly used up all his money, he was compelled for some time to turn to crime. In a complete about-face, he made wealth his goal — so he behaved just like those depraved people who do not look after their wives while they are married to them, but let them leave, and then, when their wives are married to other people, immorally try once again to seduce them. He never stopped himself from doing anything, however despicable, as long as the consequence was profit and gain. What he acquired from this was no great fortune, but, quite soon, a very extensive reputation for iniquity. The chief source of his notoriety, however, was a response that the oracle of Amphilochus gave him.

Apparently, he had sent to ask the god whether he would live a better life in the future. The god replied that he would be better off when he died. Now, in a sense, this is exactly what happened to him a short while later. He fell from a height onto his head, and although there was no wound, only a bruise, he seemed to be dead. And then two days later, when he was actually just about to be buried, he came to. Once he was well and normal again, which did not take long, he transformed his life beyond recognition. In fact, he is acknowledged by the Cilicians to have been the most honest businessman of his times, and they know of no one who was more religious or who caused his enemies more distress or was a truer friend. The upshot was that everyone who met him wanted to hear the reason for the change, since they imagined that so thorough a reorganization of character could not be due to any banal circumstances. And they were quite right, as he himself explained to Protogenes and other equally good friends of his.

When his spirit was expelled from his body, at first, he said, the transformation made him feel like a helmsman might feel if he were thrown overboard from his ship into the depths of the sea. Next, he rose upwards a little way, and seemed then to be breathing as a whole and to be seeing in all directions around himself, as if his soul were a single open eye. What he was seeing, however, was not what he had been seeing before, except for the stars — but they were huge and at immense distances from one another and were emitting light that was not only an amazing color, but also had energy, which allowed his soul to ride the light as evenly as a ship on calm water and to travel everywhere easily and swiftly. He omitted a great deal of what he saw and went on to say that when the souls of the dead come up from below, they form a fiery bubble as they cleave the air, then, when the bubble gently bursts, the souls emerge in human form, but in miniature. They do not all move uniformly: some of the souls leap out of the bubble with incredible lightness and shoot upwards in a straight line, others behave like spindles and whirl around in a circle while at the same time tending sometimes in a downward direction and sometimes in an upward direction, and so move in an untidy and chaotic spiral and take a very long time before eventually quieting down. The majority of the souls were strangers, but he saw two or three of his acquaintances and tried to communicate with them and talk to them. They did not hear him, however, and were behaving unusually: they were frantically and frenetically trying to avoid being seen or touched. At first they darted about here and there on their own, but later they met plenty of other souls in the same state and clung to them, and the whole mass moved all over the place aimlessly, making meaningless noises mixed up with sounds like exclamations of grief and terror. There was another set of souls, high up in the pure part of the atmosphere, who looked radiant, and when they approached one another, which they did often, it was out of affection. However, they kept away from the other, distracted souls. Apparently, they indicated their repugnance by contracting into themselves and their pleasure and approval by expanding and spreading out.

He said that he recognized one of these souls as that of a relative, but only just recognized him, since he had died when he was a child. This soul came up close to him and said, "Hello, Thespesius."

He was astonished and said that he was not Thespesius, but Aridaeus.

"You may have been Aridaeus before," replied his relative, "but from now on you are Thespesius, 'godlike.' You see, you have not actually died: the gods have allowed you to come here with your intelligence, but with the rest of your soul left behind in your body like an anchor. If now or at any time in the future you need evidence of this, here it is: the souls of the dead do not cast a shadow, and they do not blink their eyes."

These words caused Thespesius to use his rational mind to pull himself together to a greater degree, and he looked and saw that whereas he had a vague, shadowy line, which swayed in time with him, the others were surrounded by an aura of light and were transparent. They were not all identical, however. Some emitted light of a single, even, constant, uniform intensity, as the full moon does when it is at its most pure. Others had intermittent patches or occasional welts; others were extraordinary to look at, since they were blotchy all over, marked with freckles like vipers. And others had faint scratch marks.

Thespesius's relative (there is no reason not to refer to people's souls by name in this way) proceeded to give a detailed account of everything. He said that the role of chief punisher of wrongdoing of every kind has been given to Adrasteia, the daughter of Necessity and Zeus, and that no criminal, however grand or insignificant, can use anonymity or dominance to escape her. There are three kinds of punishment, and each has its own custodian and agent. Swift Poiné takes care of those who are punished without delay and whose punishment is entirely physical. She acts gently, in a sense, and leaves a lot of residual impurities. People whose iniquity is more difficult to heal are handed over by their deity to Diké after their death. The third and most savage of the assistants of Adrasteia is Erinys, who, once Diké has rejected them, takes on those who are altogether incurable. She hounds them as they wander here and there, trying to hide. She exterminates them all, in a variety of brutal and cruel ways, and imprisons them in the place that has no identity or form.

"As for the first two types of punishment," he went on, "the one administered by Poiné, which takes place while the criminal is still alive, resembles certain punishments employed by foreigners, in Persia, for instance. One form of punishment entails the depilation and whipping of the clothes and headgear of people who are being punished, who weep and beg for the punishment to end. Analogously, punishments that involve people's property or bodies make no telling contact and fail to address the actual iniquity, but are usually aimed at people's reputations and how they are perceived.

Anyone who gets from there to here without having been punished and purified falls into the hands of Diké. His soul is exposed and naked. There is nowhere for him to slink away to. He is incapable of covering up and concealing his wickedness, but everything about him is utterly plain for all to see. If either of his parents or any of his ancestors were good, she shows him first to them, so that they can see how contemptible and despicable he is. If they were bad, he watches them being punished — and they can see him watching — before his own extensive punishment, in which each of his emotions is stripped from him. This ordeal involves agony that is so overwhelming and excruciating that it exceeds the pain of corporal punishment to the same extent that actual pain would be more real than dreaming about it. The scars and welts which each of the emotions entail are more permanent in some cases than in others.

And," he continued, "have a look at the variety and diversity of ways in which the souls are colored. One is drab and dirty, smeared with stinginess and cupidity. Another is the red of blood or fire, thanks to his viciousness and cruelty. Grey always signifies that hedonistic self-indulgence has proved difficult to eradicate. Just as blackness is what squid discharge, the presence of spite and malice produces the venomous, pus-like green you see over there. These colors are the result of iniquity down there on earth, when the soul is modified by the emotions and in turn modifies what the body does. Here, on the other hand, the complete obliteration of these colors, and the soul's gaining a single, lucid hue, are the culmination of purification and punishment. But as long as the colors are there, then the emotions recur with all their turbulence and excitation, which is faint and quickly extinguished in some souls, but in others has a vigorous intensity.

After repeated doses of chastisement, some of these souls regain their proper condition and state, but others are returned to the bodies of living creatures by the violence of their incomprehension and indiscriminate hedonism. One soul, because its rational faculty is weak and it has never practiced the contemplation of truth, is pulled towards incarnation by its need for action. Another needs an instrument for indulgence and longs to weave together its desires with their gratification and to satisfy them with the help of the body, since here all that is available is an incomplete shadow, a phantom pleasure, that can never be fulfilled."

Here he stopped talking, and Thespesius was guided by him easily and unerringly over what seemed to be a vast region....

Their next stop was to see people being punished. At first, this was simply a distressing and pitiful sight, but then Thespesius started to come across friends, relatives, and acquaintances being punished, and this was a shock. They were suffering terribly and being punished in demeaning and agonizing ways. They cried out pitifully and mournfully to him. Finally, he saw his own father emerging out of a pit, marked and scarred all over, and reaching for him with his hands. The overseers of his father's punishments allowed him no secrets. They forced him to admit that he had foully poisoned some visitors for their money. On earth, no one had suspected him, but here he had been found out. He had already suffered, and now was being taken away for more.

Thespesius was so scared and terrified that he did not dare beg or plead for mercy for his father, but just wanted to turn and run away. But he could not see the gentle relative who had been his guide; instead, other deities, who were frightening to look at, were pushing him forward, as if to say that he had no choice but to continue exploring everything. He noticed that anyone whose crimes had been immediately detected and punished was not now having to endure severe torment here or be oppressed to the same degree, since all that remained to be dealt with was his irrational, emotional aspect. However, those who had spent their lives without their iniquity being detected, because they covered themselves with a screen and a semblance of goodness, were hemmed in by guards of a different kind, who harassed and tormented them until they forced them to turn their souls inside out with ghastly wriggles and convolutions, which were reminiscent of how lugworms turn themselves inside out when they swallow a hook. The guards flayed and cut open some of them, who were carrying their wickedness in their rational, authoritative part, to reveal them as infected and spotty.

And he said that he saw other souls entwined, snake-like, in groups of two or three or more, who were eating one another because they held a grudge or felt vindictive about things that had been done to them or that they had done during their lifetimes. There was also a row of pools, one of boiling gold, another of freezing lead, and a third of rough iron. The deities in charge of these pools used implements, like blacksmiths', alternately to lift souls up and then lower them — these were the souls of people whose criminality stemmed from greed and avarice. When the souls had been heated up in the golden pool until they became transparent from the heat, the deities dropped them into the pool of lead for tempering. They immediately froze as hard as hailstones, and then the deities transferred them to the iron pool. Here they became hideously black, and they were so hard that bits of them were chipped and broken off, and their shapes became distorted. And then they were taken back to the gold pool again. These metamorphoses caused them excruciating pain, Thespesius said.

The souls whose suffering aroused the most pity, he said, were those whose debt had been inherited by descendants or children, because they were under the impression that they had been absolved from repayment but were then apprehended at a later date. What happened was that whenever any of their descendants or children arrived there and came across the soul of their forebear, they assaulted him furiously, yelling and screaming. They showed him the evidence of their suffering and cursed him and chased him around — and he could not escape and hide, however much he wanted to. Before long, the avenging deities were hunting him down and rushing him off for his original punishment, and he would go off wailing, because he already knew what penalty he was facing. And Thespesius said that some of these souls were swarming with descendants, who clung to them exactly like bees or bats and emitted piercing cries in anger at the memory of the pain they had endured because of them.

The last thing he saw was the souls being modified for rebirth. They were being wrenched and reshaped into all kinds of living creatures by specialist artisans, who were using a combination of tools and blows to join and force together some parts, twist others back, and obliterate and eliminate others altogether, so as to make the souls fit different characteristics and ways of life. And he saw among the others Nero's soul, which was in a bad way, not least because it had been run through with red-hot nails. The artisans had a form already prepared for him — that of the Nicander's viper, in which he would live once, as a fetus, he had eaten his way out of his mother, but suddenly he said, an intense light blazed forth, and a voice arose from the light, ordering them to transfer Nero's soul to another, more inoffensive species by fashioning the form of a musical animal that could live near marshes and ponds. For, the voice announced, he had already been punished for his crimes, and moreover the gods owed him a favor for freeing the nation that, of all those he ruled, was the best and the most favored by the gods.

Up to this point, he had been a spectator, but he was poised to turn back when he became paralyzed with fear. A woman of incredible beauty and size had grabbed hold of him, and she said, "Come here, you. This will help you remember everything better." And she was bringing a red-hot stick, like painters use, up close to him. Another woman stopped her, however, and he was jerked away as suddenly as if he had been fired from a bowstring by an extremely tempestuous and strong wind. He landed on his body and looked up almost from his actual grave.

14. DESCRIPTION OF GREECE[14]

BY PAUSANIUS (110–c. 180 CE)

Greek, late 2nd Century CE

The other part of the picture, the one on the left, shows Odysseus, who has descended into what is called Hades to inquire of the soul of Teiresias about his safe return home. The objects depicted are as follow. There is water like a river, clearly intended for Acheron, with reeds growing in it. The forms of the fishes appear so dim that you will take them to be shadows rather than fish. On the river is a boat with the ferryman at the oars.

Polygnotus followed, I think, the poem called the *Minyad*. For in this poem occur lines referring to Theseus and Peirithous: "Then the boat on which embark the dead, that the old ferryman, Charon, used to steer, they found not within its moorings." For this reason then Polygnotus too painted Charon as a man well stricken in years.

Those on board the boat are not altogether distinguished. Tellis appears as a youth in years, and Cleoboea as still a maiden, holding on her knees a chest such as they are wont to make for Demeter. All I heard about Tellis was that Archilochus the poet was his grandson, while as for Cleoboea, they say that she was the first to bring the orgies of Demeter to Thasos from Paros.

On the bank of Acheron there is a notable group under the boat of Charon, consisting of a man who had been undutiful to his father and is now being throttled by him. For the men of old held their parents in the greatest respect, as we may infer, among other instances, from those in Catania called the Pious, who, when the fire flowed down on Catania from Aetna, held of no account gold or silver, but when they fled took up, one his mother and another his father. As they struggled on, the fire rushed up and caught them in the flames. Not even so would they put down their parents, and it is said that the stream of lava divided itself in two, and the fire passed on, doing no hurt to either young men or their parents. These Catanians even at the present day receive honors from their fellow countrymen.

In Polygnotus's picture, near to the man who maltreated his father and for this drinks his cup of woe in Hades, is a man who paid the penalty for sacrilege. The woman who is punishing him is skilled in poisonous and other drugs.

So it appears that in those days men laid the greatest stress on piety to the gods, as the Athenians showed when they took the sanctuary of Olympian Zeus at Siracusa. They moved none of the offerings, but left the Siracusan priest as their keeper. Datis the Persian too showed his piety in his address to the Delians, and in this act as well, when having found an image of Apollo in a Phoenician ship, he restored it to the Tanagraeans at Delium. So at that time all men held the divine in reverence, and this is why Polygnotus has depicted the punishment of him who committed sacrilege.

Higher up than the figures I have enumerated comes Eurynomus, said by the Delphian guides to be one of the demons in Hades, who eats off all the flesh of the corpses, leaving only their bones. But Homer's *Odyssey*, the poem called the *Minyad*, and the *Returns*, although they tell of Hades and its horrors, know of no demon called Eurynomus. However, I will describe what he is like and his attitude in the painting. He is of a color between blue and black, like that of meat flies. He is showing his teeth and is seated, and under him is spread a vulture's skin.

Next after Eurynomus are Auge of Arcadia and Iphimedeia. Auge visited the house of Teuthras in Mysia, and of all the women with whom Heracles is said to have mated, none gave birth to a son more like his father than she did. Great honors are paid to Iphimedeia by the Carians in Mylasa.

Higher up than the figures I have already enumerated are Perimedes and Eurylochus, the companions of Odysseus, carrying victims for sacrifice. These are black rams. After them is a man seated, said by the inscription to be Ocnus [Sloth]. He is depicted as plaiting a cord, and by him stands a she-ass, eating up the cord as quickly as it is plaited. They say that this Ocnus was a diligent man with an extravagant wife. Everything he earned by working was quickly spent by his wife.

So they will have it that Polygnotus has painted a parable about the wife of Ocnus. I know also that the Ionians, whenever they see a man labouring at nothing profitable, say that such a one is plaiting the cord of Ocnus. Ocnus too is the name given to a bird by the seers who observe birds that are ominous. This Ocnus is the largest and most beautiful of the herons, a rare bird if ever there was one.

Tityus too is in the picture; he is no longer being punished, but has been reduced to nothing by continuous torture, an indistinct and mutilated phantom.

…

After Callisto and the women with her is the form of a cliff, and Sisyphus, the son of Aeolus, is trying his hardest to push the rock up it.

…

There is also in the painting a jar and an old man with a boy and two women. One of these, who is young, is under the rock. The other is beside the old man and of a like age to his. The others are carrying water, but you will guess that the old woman's water-jar is broken. All that remains of the water in the sherd, she is pouring out again into the jar. We inferred that these people too were of those who had held of no account the rites at Eleusis. For the Greeks of an earlier period looked upon the Eleusinian mysteries as being as much higher than all other religious acts as gods are higher than heroes.

Under this jar is Tantalus, enduring all the pains that Homer speaks of, and in addition the terror of the stone that hangs over him. Polygnotus has plainly followed the account of Archilochus, but I do not know whether Archilochus borrowed from others the story of the stone or whether it was an invention of his that he introduced into his poem.

So great is the number of the figures and so many are their beauties, in this painting by the Thasian artist.

15. The Golden Ass[15]

by Apuleius (124–170 ce)

Roman, late 2nd Century ce

…Then Venus spoke to Psyche again saying: "Do you see the top of that great hill, there where waters of a black and deadly color run down, nourishing the floods of the Styx and Cocytus? I charge you to go there and bring me a vessel of that water." And she gave her a crystal urn, while menacing her and threatening her terribly.

Then poor Psyche went quickly to the top of the mountain, expecting to end her life, rather than to fetch any water, because when she had come up to the ridge of the hill, she saw that it was impossible to accomplish this: for she saw a great rock gushing forth the most horrible torrents of water, which cascaded down and fell from ledge to ledge and through chasms into the valley below. On each side she saw great monsters stretching out their long and bloody necks. They never slept but were appointed to watch the river there. Even the waters seemed to be saying, "Depart! Away! What are you doing here? Fly, flee, or else you will be murdered." Then Psyche — seeing that the whole thing was impossible — stood still as if she were transformed to stone. Here body was there, and yet because of the danger confronting her, she was without sense or spirit, so that she was unable even to console herself.

But great Jupiter, remembered the service he had once done as a royal eagle when, instigated by Cupid, he brought the Phrygian boy Ganymede up to the heavens to become his own cupbearer. He thought he would offer the same service to Cupid wife's and descended from the high-house of the heavens. He said to Psyche, "O simple, naive woman, do you think you can scoop up any drop of this dreadful water? No, no. Be assured that you will never able to get near it. The gods themselves dreadfully fear even the sight of it. Haven't you heard that it is a custom among men to swear by the power of the gods, and the gods to swear by the power of the river Styx? Give me your bottle," and suddenly he took it and filled it with water from the river, and he flew past those horribly cruel monsters and brought it to Psyche, who rejoiced and presented it to Venus. But Venus would not be appeased, and menacing Psyche more and more she said, "It seems to me that you are a real witch and enchantress to accomplish these things, but this will be the end of it. Take this box and go to hell to Proserpina and ask her to send me a little of her beauty, as much as will serve me for the length of a day, and say whatever I had has been eaten away since my son fell sick. But return again quickly, for I have to dress myself with it and go to the theater of the gods."

Then poor Psyche perceived the end of all fortune, thinking, and not without cause, that she truly would never return since now she was compelled to go into the pit and wrath of hell. Therefore without any further delay, she went up to a high tower to throw herself down headlong — thinking that it was the best and quickest way to hell — but the tower, as if inspired, spoke to her saying, "O poor miserable wretch, why are you going to kill yourself? Why do you rashly give in to your final last peril and danger? You know that if your spirit is once separated from your body, you will surely go to hell, but never to return again. So listen to me. Sparta, a city in Greece, is not far from here. Go there and ask for the hill of Taenarus, wherein you will find a hole leading to hell, even to the Palace of Pluto, but be careful not to go empty handed to that place of darkness, but carry in your hands two cakes of barley meal soaked in wine and honey and two coins in your mouth. And when you have gone a good part of that way, you will see a lame donkey carrying wood and a lame fellow leading him. He will ask you to give him the sticks that have fallen down, but pass him by and do nothing. Little by little you will come to a river of death, where Charon is ferryman. He carries the souls over the river in his boat, but first he must be paid — you can see how avarice reigns among the dead: neither Charon nor Pluto will do any thing for nothing. If it is a poor man who wants to pass over and he hasn't the money, he'll be forced to die before they help him. So hand over to stinking Charon one of the coins that you carry for your fare, and let him take it out of your mouth. And soon you will be sitting in the boat, and you will see an old man swimming in the river, who will hold up his decaying hands and ask you to help him into the boat, but disregard him. When you've passed over to the other side, you will see some old women spinning, who will ask you to help them, but don't give in to them, because they and the others are set as baits and traps by Venus to make you drop one of your cakes. Don't think that the cakes are a trivial thing, for if you lose one of them you'll be guaranteed never to return again to this world. Next you will see an enormous and strange dog with three heads that bark continually at the souls that enter there, but he can't do them any harm. He lies day and night before Proserpina's gate and guards Pluto's house very diligently. If you throw him one of your cakes, you will gain access to Proserpina without any danger. She will welcome you and entertain you with delicate meat and drink, but sit on the ground and ask for brown bread. Then tell her your message, and when you've received the beauty that she gives, appease the dog's rage again with the other cake, and give the other coin to covetous Charon, and come back again into the world the same way as you went, but above all else take care not to look in the box. Don't be curious about the treasure of the divine beauty."

This is how the tower spoke to Psyche and warned her what she should do. Immediately she took two coins, two cakes, and everything else that she needed and went to Taenarus to enter hell.

After that Psyche passed by the lame donkey, paid her coin for passage, ignored the old man in the river, declined to help the woman spinning, and filled the ravenous month of the dog with a cake, she came to Proserpina's chamber. There Psyche would not sit on any royal seat, nor eat any delicate meat, but knelt at Proserpina's feet, content with just coarse bread. Finally she divulged her message. After she secured the magical secret in her box, she departed. She stopped the dog's mouth with the other cake and paid the boatman the other coin.

When Psyche returned from hell, to the light of the world, she was overcome by a great desire, saying, "Wouldn't I be a fool knowing that I carried here divine beauty, and did not take a little to decorate my face, thereby to please my love?" And of course, she opened the box where she saw neither beauty nor any thing else, except only infernal and deadly sleep, which immediately overcame every part of her as soon as the box was opened. And so she fell upon the ground and lay there like a sleeping corpse.

16. THE TRUE HISTORY[16]

BY LUCIAN OF SAMOSATA (120–90 CE)

Greek/Romano-Syrian, late 2nd Century CE

Rhadamanthus sent on board with me the ferryman Nauplius, who, in case we were driven on to the islands, might secure us from seizure by guaranteeing that our destination was different. As soon as our progress brought us out of the scented air, it was succeeded by a horrible smell as of bitumen, brimstone, and pitch all burning together. Mingled with this were the disgusting and intolerable fumes of roasting human flesh. The air was dark and thick, distilling a pitchy dew upon us. We could also hear the crack of whips and the yelling of many voices.

We only touched at one island, on which we also landed. It was completely surrounded by precipitous cliffs, arid, stony, rugged, treeless, unwatered. We contrived to clamber up the rocks and advanced along a track beset with thorns and snags — a hideous scene. When we reached the prison and the place of punishment, what first drew our wonder was the character of the whole. The very ground stood thick with a crop of knife blades and pointed stakes, and it was ringed round with rivers, one of slime, a second of blood, and the innermost of flame. This last was very broad and quite impassable. The flame flowed like water, swelled like the sea, and teemed with fish, some resembling firebrands, and others, the small ones, live coals. These were called lamplets.

One narrow way led across all three. Its gate was kept by Timon of Athens. Nauplius secured us admission, however, and then we saw the chastisement of many kings and many common men. Some were known to us. Indeed there hung Cinyras, swinging in eddies of smoke. Our guides described the life and guilt of each culprit. The severest torments were reserved for those who in life had been liars and written false history. The class was numerous and included Ctesias of Cnidus and Herodotus. The fact was an encouragement to me, knowing that I had never told a lie.

I soon found the sight more than I could bear and returning to the ship bade farewell to Nauplius and resumed the voyage.

17. MENIPPUS[17]

BY LUCIAN OF SAMOSATA (120–90 CE)

Greek / Romano-Syrian, late 2nd Century CE

Menippus: …Well, day was just beginning to break when we went down to the river and set about getting under way. He had provided a boat, victims, mead, and everything else that we should need for the ritual. So we shipped all the stores, and at length ourselves.

"Gloomily hied us aboard, with great tears falling profusely." (*Odyssey* 11.5)

For a space we drifted along in the river, and then we sailed into the marsh and the lake in which the Euphrates loses itself. After crossing this, we came to a deserted, woody, sunless place. There at last we landed with Mithrobarzanes leading the way. We dug a pit, we slaughtered the sheep, and we sprinkled their blood about it. Meanwhile the magician held a burning torch and no longer muttered in a low tone but shouted as loudly as he could, invoking the spirits, one and all, at the top of his lungs; also the Tormentors, the Furies, "Hecate, queen of the night, and eerie Persephoneia."

With these names he intermingled a number of foreign-sounding, meaningless words of many syllables.

In a trice the whole region began to quake, the ground was rent asunder by the incantation. The barking of Cerberus was audible afar off, and things took on a monstrously gloomy and sullen look.

"Aye, deep down it affrighted the king of the dead, Aidoneus" (*Iliad* 20.61) for by that time we could see almost everything — the lake, and the river of burning fire, and the palace of Pluto. But in spite of it all, we went down through the chasm, finding Rhadamanthus, almost dead of fright. Cerberus barked a bit, to be sure, and stirred slightly, but when I hastily touched my lyre he was at

85

once bewitched by the music. When we reached the lake, however, we came near not getting across, for the ferry was already crowded and full of groaning. Only wounded men were aboard, one injured in the leg, another in the head, and so on. They were there, in my opinion, through some war or other.

However, when good old Charon saw the lion-skin he thought that I was Heracles, so he took me in, and not only ferried me across gladly but pointed out the path for us when we went ashore. Since we were in the dark, Mithrobarzanes led the way and I followed after, keeping hold of him, until we reached a very large meadow overgrown with asphodel, where the shades of the dead flitted squeaking about us. Going ahead little by little, we came to the court of Minos. As it chanced, he himself was sitting on a lofty throne, while beside him stood the Tormentors, the Furies, and the Avengers. From one side a great number of men were being led up in line, bound together with a long chain. They were said to be adulterers, procurers, tax-collectors, toadies, informers, and all that crowd of people who create such confusion in life. In a separate company the millionaires and the money-lenders came up, pale, pot-bellied, and gouty, each of them with a neck-iron and a hundred-pound "crow" upon him. Standing by, we looked at what was going on and listened to the pleas of the defendants, who were prosecuted by speakers of a novel and surprising sort.

Friend: Who were they, in heaven's name? Don't hesitate to tell me that also.

Menippus: You know these shadows that our bodies cast in the sunshine?

Friend: Why, to be sure!

Menippus: Well, when we die, they prefer charges and give evidence against us, exposing whatever we have done in our lives. And they are considered very trustworthy because they always keep us company and never leave our bodies.

But to resume, Minos would examine each man carefully and send him away to the Place of the Wicked, to be punished in proportion to his crimes. And he dealt most harshly with those who were swollen with pride of wealth and place and almost expected men to bow down and worship them, for he resented their short-lived vainglory and superciliousness and their failure to remember that they themselves were mortal and had become possessed of mortal goods. So, after stripping off all their quondam splendor — wealth, I mean, and lineage and sovereignty — they stood there naked with hanging heads, reviewing, point by point, their happy life among us as if it had been a dream. For my part I was highly delighted to see that, and whenever I recognized one of them, I would go up and quietly remind him what he used to be in life and how puffed up he had been then, when many men stood at his portals in the early morning awaiting his advent, hustled about, and locked out by his servants, while he himself, bursting upon their vision at last in garments of purple or gold or gaudy stripes, thought that he was conferring happiness and bliss upon those who greeted him if he proffered his right hand or his breast to be covered with kisses. They chafed, I assure you, as they listened!

But to return to Minos, he gave one decision by favor, for Dionysius of Sicily had been charged with many dreadful and impious crimes by Dion as prosecutor and the shadow as witness, but Aristippus of Cyrene appeared — they hold him in honor, and he has very great influence among the people of the lower world — and when Dionysius was within an ace of being chained up to the Chimera, he got him let off from the punishment by saying that many men of letters had found him obliging in the matter of money.

Leaving the court reluctantly, we came to the place of punishment, where in all truth, my friend, there were many pitiful things to hear and to see. The sound of scourges could be heard and therewithal the wails of those roasting on the fire. There were racks and pillories and wheels. Chimera tore and Cerberus ravened. They were being punished all together, kings, slaves, satraps, poor, rich, and beggars, and all were sorry for their excesses. Some of them we even recognized when we saw them, all that were recently dead. But they covered their faces and turned away, and if they so much as cast a glance at us, it was thoroughly servile and obsequious, even though they had been unimaginably oppressive and haughty in life. Poor people, however, were getting only half as much torture and resting at intervals before being punished again. Moreover, I saw all that is told of in the legends — Ixion, Sisyphus, Tantalus the Phrygian, who was certainly in a bad way, and earthborn Tityus — Heracles, how big he was! Indeed, he took up land enough for a farm as he lay there!

After making our way past these people also, we entered the Acherusian Plain, where we found the demigods and the fair women and the whole crowd of the dead, living by nations and by clans, some of them ancient and moldy, and, as Homer says, "impalpable," while others were still well preserved and substantial, particularly the Egyptians, thanks to the durability of their embalming process. It was not at all easy, though, to tell them apart, for all, without exception, become precisely alike when their bones are bare. However, with some difficulty and by dint of long study we made them out. But they were lying one atop of another, ill-defined, unidentified, retaining no longer any trace of earthly beauty. So, with many skeletons lying together, all alike staring horridly and vacuously and baring their teeth, I questioned myself how I could distinguish Thersites from handsome Nireus, or the mendicant Irus from the king of the Phaeacians, or the cook Pyrrhias from Agamemnon; for none of their former means of identification abode with them, but their bones were all alike, undefined, unlabeled, and unable ever again to be distinguished by anyone....

Friend: But tell me, Menippus; those who have such expensive, high monuments on earth, and tombstones and statues and inscriptions — are they no more highly honored there than common dead?

Menippus: Nonesense, man! If you had seen Mausolus himself — I mean Carian, so famous for his monument — I know right well that you would never have stopped laughing, so humbly did he lie where he was flung, in a cubby-hole, inconspicuous among the rest of the plebeian dead, deriving, in my opinion, only this much satisfaction from his monument, that he was heavy laden with such a great weight resting upon him. When Aeacus measures off the space for each, my friend — and he gives at most not over a foot — one must be content to lie in it, huddled together to fit its compass. But you would have laughed much more heartily, I think, if you had seen our kings and satraps reduced to poverty there, and either selling salt fish on account of their neediness or teaching the alphabet, and getting abused and hit over the head by all comers, like the meanest of slaves. In fact, when I saw Philip of Macedon, I could not control my laughter. He was pointed out to me in a corner, cobbling worn-out sandals for pay! Many others, too, could be seen begging at cross-roads — your Xerxeses, I mean, and Dariuses and Polycrateses.

Friend: What you say about the kings is extraordinary and almost incredible. But what was Socrates doing, and Diogenes, and the rest of the wise men?

Menippus: As to Socrates, there too he goes about cross-questioning everyone. His associates are Palamedes, Odysseus, Nestor, and other talkative corpses. His legs, I may say, were still puffed up and swollen from his draught of poison. And good old Diogenes lives with Sardanapalus the Assyrian, Midas the Phrysian, and several other wealthy men. As he hears them lamenting and reviewing their former good-fortune, he laughs and rejoices; and often he lies on his back and sings in a very harsh and unpleasant voice, drowning out their lamentations, so that the gentlemen are annoyed and think of changing their lodgings because they cannot stand Diogenes.

Friend: Well, enough of this, but what was the motion that in the beginning you said had been passed against the rich?

Menippus: Thanks for reminding me. Somehow or other, in spite of my intention to speak about that, I went very much astray in my talk.

During my stay there, the city fathers called a public meeting to discuss matters of general interest, so when I saw many people running in the same direction, I mingled with the dead and speedily became one of the electors myself. Well, various business was transacted, and at last that about the rich. After many dreadful charges of violence and mendacity and superciliousness and injustice had been brought against them, at length one of the demagogues rose and read the following motion.

Motion:"Whereas many lawless deeds are done in life by the rich, who plunder and oppress and in every way humiliate the poor,

"Be it resolved by the senate and people, that when they die their bodies be punished like those of the other malefactors, but their souls be sent back up into life and enter into donkeys until they shall have passed two hundred and fifty thousand years in the said condition, transmigrating from donkey to donkey, bearing burdens and being driven by the poor; and that thereafter it be permitted them to die.

"On motion of Scully Fitzbones of Corpsebury, Cadavershire."

After his motion had been read, the officials put it to the vote, the majority indicated assent by the usual sign,

Brimo brayed and Cerberus howled. That is the way in which their motions are enacted and ratified.

Well, there you have what took place at the meeting. For my part, I did what I came to do. Going to Teiresias, I told him the whole story and besought him to tell me what sort of life he considered the best. He laughed — he is a blind little old gentleman, pale, with a piping voice — and said: "My son, I know the reason for your perplexity. It came from the wise men who are not consistent with themselves. But it is not permissible to tell you, for Rhadamanthus has forbidden it." "Don't say that, gaffer," said I. "Tell me, and don't allow me to go about in life blinder than you are." So he took me aside, and after he had led me a good way apart from the others, he bent his head slightly toward my ear and said: "The life of the common sort is best, and you will act more wisely if you stop speculating about heavenly bodies and discussing final causes and first causes, spit your scorn at those clever syllogisms, and counting all that sort of thing nonsense, make it always your sole object to put the present to good use and to hasten on your way, laughing a great deal and taking nothing seriously."

"So he spoke, and betook him again through the asphodel meadow." (*Odyssey* 11.539)

As it was late by then, I said: "Come, Mithrobarzanes, why do we delay? Why not go back to life again?" To this he replied: "Never fear, Menippus. I will show you a quick and easy short cut." And then, taking me to a place murkier than the rest of the region and pointing with his finger to a dim and slender ray of light coming in as if from a keyhole, a long way off, he said: "That is the sanctuary of Trophonius, where the people from Boetia come down. So go up by that route and you will be in Greece directly." Delighted with his words, I embraced the sorcerer, very laboriously crawled up through the hole somehow, and found myself in Lebadeia.

8.   Charon welcoming a shade. Attic Greek red-figure
(white-ground) lekythos attributed to the Tymbos painter,
c. 500–450 BCE. Ashmolean Museum, Oxford. (Photo, Carole
Raddato)

NOTES

1. Based on the translation by Samuel Butler, *The Iliad of Homer* (London: Longmans, Green, and Co., 1898) and found in the Perseus Project at http://data.perseus.org/texts/urn:cts:greekLit:tlg0012.tlg001.perseus-eng2.

2. Based on the translation by Samuel Butler, *The Odyssey of Homer*, edited by Timothy Power and Gregory Nagy (London: Longmans, Green, and Co., 1900) as found in the Perseus Project at http://data.perseus.org/texts/urn:cts:greekLit:tlg0012.tlg002.perseus-eng2.

3. Lines 714–819. Adapted from Hesiod, *The Homeric Hymns and Homerica* with an English translation by Hugh G. Evelyn-White (Cambridge, MA: Harvard University Press; London, William Heinemann Ltd., 1914.) From Perseus Project: http://data.perseus.org/texts/urn:cts:greekLit:tlg0020.tlg001.perseus-eng1.

4. From "Hymn 2 to Demeter (Demeter I)," lines c. 78–82, 334–49, 258–69, 480–84, in Anonymous. *The Homeric Hymns and Homerica* with an English translation by Hugh G. Evelyn-White. Homeric Hymns. (Cambridge, MA: Harvard University Press; London, William Heinemann Ltd. 1914) and at http://data.perseus.org/texts/urn:cts:greekLit:tlg0013.tlg002.perseus-eng1.

5. Excerpted from ll. 136–52, 180–206, 269–311, 462–78, 549–78, 605–73, Aristophanes, *The Peace, The Birds, The Frogs,* translated by Benjamin Bickley Rogers (Cambridge, MA: Harvard University Press; London: William Heinemann, Ltd., 1924), 309–57 and at http://classics.mit.edu/Aristophanes/frogs.html.

6. Translated from the Italian translation published in Giovanni Pugliese Carratelli, *Le Lamine d'oro orfiche,* (Milan: Adelphi, 2001), 40-41 and reproduced in the descriptive materials at the Museo Archeologico Statale di Vibo Valentia. See also Alberto Bernabé and Ana Isabel

Jiménez San Cristobal, *Instructions for the Netherworld: The Orphic Gold Tablets* (Leiden: Brill, 2008), 9–10.

7. Lines 523a–526b in Plato, *Plato in Twelve Volumes,* Vol. 3, translated by W.R.M. Lamb (Cambridge, MA: Harvard University Press; London: William Heinemann Ltd., 1967). From Perseus http://data.perseus.org/texts/ urn:cts:greekLit:tlg0059.tlg023.perseus-eng1. This work is licensed under a Creative Commons Attribution-ShareAlike 3.0 United States License (https:// creativecommons.org/licenses/by-sa/3.0/us/).

8. Lines 111e–114c. Plato, *Plato in Twelve Volumes,* Vol. 1, translated by Harold North Fowler, introduction by W.R.M. Lamb (Cambridge, MA: Harvard University Press; London, William Heinemann Ltd., 1966). From Perseus http://data.perseus.org/texts/urn:cts:greekLit:tlg0059. tlg004.perseus-eng1. This work is licensed under a Creative Commons Attribution-ShareAlike 3.0 United States License (https://creativecommons.org/licenses/ by-sa/3.0/us/).

9. Lines 10.614b–616b, Plato, *Plato in Twelve Volumes,* Vol. 5 & 6, translated by Paul Shorey, introduction by W.R.M. Lamb (Cambridge, MA: Harvard University Press; London, William Heinemann Ltd., 1969). From Perseus http://data.perseus.org/texts/urn:cts:greekLit:tlg0059. tlg030.perseus-eng1. This work is licensed under a Creative Commons Attribution-ShareAlike 3.0 United States License (https://creativecommons.org/licenses/ by-sa/3.0/us/).

10. From Virgil, *Aeneid,* translated by Theodore C. Williams (Boston: Houghton Mifflin Co., 1908), 191–95, 197–208, 211–13; 1910 edition online at http://data.perseus.org/ texts/urn:cts:latinLit:phi0690.phi003.perseus-eng2. Lines 236–331, 384–629, and 703–51.

11. Adapted from Book 10, lines 10–63, of Ovid's *Metamorphoses*, translated by Brookes More (Boston: Cornhill Publishing Co., 1922).

12. From Lucius Annaeus Seneca, *Tragedies*, translated by Frank Justus Miller (Cambridge, MA: Harvard University Press, 1917), 139–49. https://en.wikisource.org/wiki/Tragedies_of_Seneca_(1907)_Miller/Hercules_Furens.

13. Adapted and excerpted from http://qdj.50megs.com/PlutarchVision.html. Translation by Robert Waterhouse, 1992. Also available in Plutach, *Moralia*, edited by G.P. Goold, translated by Phillip H. De Lacy and Benedict Einarson, Loeb Classical Library (Cambridge, MA: Harvard University Press, 1959), 7: 269–99.

14. Excerpts of Book 10, chapters 28, 30.6 and 31.10–12 from Pausanias, *Description of Greece*, with an English translation by W.H.S. Jones and H.A. Ormerod, 4 vols. (Cambridge, MA: Harvard University Press; London, William Heinemann Ltd., 1918), 4: 10:28–31. http://data.perseus.org/citations/urn:cts:greekLit:tlg0525.tlg001.perseus-eng1:10.28 and ff.

15. Adapted from "The Marriage of Cupid and Psyche," in Apuleius, *The Golden Ass*, Book 22, trans. by William Adlington. http://www.gutenberg.org/files/1666/1666-h/1666-h.htm#link2H_4_0030.

15. From 2: 29–32 of Lucian of Samosata, *The True History*, translated by H.W. Fowler & F.G. Fowler (Oxford, Clarendon Press, 1905), 165–66.

17. From *Lucian*, translated by A.H. Harmon (Cambridge, MA: Harvard University Press, 1926), 4:87–109.

GLOSSARY

Achaeans, inhabitants of Achaea in the northwestern part of the Peloponnese in Greece, but for HOMER in the *Iliad* Mycenaean-era Greeks in general.

Acheron, one of the five rivers of HADES, known as the river of woe. According to some legends, the STYX and the PHLEGETHON both flowed into it; according to Virgil, it was the principal river of TARTARUS, and the Styx and the COCYTUS both issued from it.

Acherusian Lake, the lake into which the ACHERON flowed out of HADES, identified with Lake AVERNUS.

Achilles, a Greek hero of the TROJAN WAR.

Adrasteia, a nymph who was charged by Rhea with nurturing the infant ZEUS in secret in the DICTAEAN CAVE to protect him from his father CRONOS.

Aeacus, a mythological king of the island of Aegina in the SARONIC GULF. He was the father of PELEUS, Telamon, and Phocus and was the grandfather of ACHILLES and Telemonian AJAX.

Aeneas, a Trojan hero, the son of ANCHISES and the goddess VENUS. He is a hero of Rome and an ancestor of Romulus and Remus.

Agamemnon, king of Mycenae, commander of the Greek army during the TROJAN WAR. Helen of Troy was the wife of his brother Menelaus. Murdered upon his return from Troy by AIGISTHOS, the lover of his wife, Clytemnestra.

Aiakos, a mythological king of the island of Aegina in the SARONIC GULF.

Aidoneus, see HADES.

Aigisthos, Aegisthus, with his lover Clytemnestra, murdered AGAMEMNON and became king of Mycenae. Aigisthos previously murdered his uncle Atreus and put his own father on the throne of Mycenae.

Ajax, also Telemonian Ajax, a hero in the TROJAN WAR, also known as "Ajax the Great."

Alcides, an alternative name for HERAKLES.

Alcinous, according to HOMER, he is the happy ruler of the PHAEACIA, who by Arete had five sons and one daughter, Nausicaa.

Aloïdae, the handsome giants, Otus and Ephialtes, who stormed OLYMPUS to gain Artemis and HERA. They were killed by APOLLO and bound to columns in the underworld by snakes, with the nymph of the STYX in the form of an owl over them.

Amphilochus, a prominent seer of Greek mythology, who founded several oracles.

Amphrysian Priestess, the Cumaean Sibyl, who was given the power of prophecy by APOLLO and resided at Cumae, west of Naples.

Anchises, the father of AENEAS, whom he meets in the underworld.

Antilochos, the son of Nestor, king of Pylos, one of the ACHAEANS in the TROJAN WAR.

Apollo, the son of ZEUS and Leto, is known variously as a god of music, truth and prophecy, healing, the sun and light, plague, poetry, and more.

Archelaus, Herod Archelaus, the son of Herod the Great. He was the ruler of Samaria, Judea, and Idumea. According to Josephus he ordered the slaughter of 3000 Jews in the Temple in 4 BCE just before Passover.

Ardiaeos the Great, whom Plato calls a "tyrant in a certain city of PAMPHYLIA." Nothing more is known for certain.

Aristeides, an ancient Athenian statesman revered as just and honorable.

Aristippus of Cyrene, founder of a philosophical school, which taught that the goal of life was to seek pleasure by adapting circumstances to oneself and maintaining proper control over both adversity and prosperity.

Armenius, described by Plato as the father of ER, but nothing more is known about him.

Athena, the virgin patroness of Athens and the Greek goddess of wisdom, courage, inspiration, civilization, law and justice, mathematics, strength, war strategy, the arts, crafts, and skill.

Avernus, a volcanic crater, which comprises Lake Avernus, near Cumae, west of Naples. According to Roman mythology, it is an entrance to the underworld. See also ACHERUSIAN LAKE.

Bacchus, see DIONYSIUS.

Belides, see DANAIDES.

Briareos, also known as Aegaeon and Obriareos, one of the three Greek Hekatonkheires, or Hundred–handed Ones, giants of incredible strength and ferocity and children of GAIA and Uranus. They defeated the TITANS and became guards of TARTARUS. Brother of Cottus and Gyes.

Caeneus, a legendary hero of Thessaly, driven into the ground with timbers by his enemies the Centaurs. According to Ovid's *Metamorphoses*, he was originally a woman.

Callicles, an ancient political philosopher, but he may be only a character created for Plato's *Gorgias*.

Cerberia, see CERBERUS.

Cerberus, the three-headed hound of HADES who guards the gates of the underworld.

Charon, the ferryman of HADES who conducts the dead across the rivers STYX and ACHERON.

Chimera, a fire-breathing hybrid monster often comprising parts of a lion, goat, and serpent.

Cilicians, inhabitants of the coastal region of Anatolia in southwest Turkey, north and northeast of Cyprus.

Cinesias, a poet of classical Athens who, according to Aristophanes, tried to borrow a pair of bird's wings to aid his poetic inspiration.

Cinyras, a mythological king of Cyprus, who committed suicide after engaging in incest with his daughter Myrrha, fathering Adonis.

Circe, Greek goddess of magic, daughter of the sun-god Helios, renowned for her knowledge of potions and herbs.

Cocytus, a river of the underworld, known also as the river of wailing. It flows into the ACHERON.

Cottus, see BRIAREOS.

Cronos, or Kronos, in Greek mythology, a TITAN, the youngest of the first generation, who overthrew his father and ruled during the mythological Golden Age. He was eventually overthrown himself by his son ZEUS and imprisoned in TARTARUS with the other Titans, although his fate differs in different texts.

Ctesias of Cnidus, a fifth century BCE Greek physician and historian.

Cupid, The god of love and affection, son of VENUS and Mars, the god of war.

Cymopolea or Cymopoleia, the daughter of POSEIDON, thought to be the goddess of violent sea storms.

Danaans, one of the names for the Greeks used in HOMER's *Iliad* and *Odyssey*.

Danaides, the fifty daughters of DANAUS, who were married to the fifty sons of his brother Aegyptus. They promised their father to cut off the heads of their husbands on their wedding night, and only one or two failed to carry out the deed. Although in some versions of their legend they are purified, in others they are condemned to HADES where they everlastingly pour water into a vessel full of holes.

Danaus, in Greek mythology, the twin brother of Aegyptus, a mythical king of Egypt. Danaus was the father of fifty daughters, the DANAIDES.

Day, see HEMERA.

Death, see THANATOS.

Delos, a sacred Mediterranean island in the Cyclades known as the birthplace of APOLLO and Artemis.

Demeter, a Greek fertility goddess, mother of Persephone.

Dictaean Cave, a sacred cave in eastern Crete, considered a birthplace of Zeus.

Dido, also Elissa, founder and first queen of Carthage, daughter of the king of Tyre, brother to Pygmalion and wife to Sichaeus, or Acerbas.

Diké, the Greek goddess of justice and judgment, the spirit of moral order.

Diomus, a favorite attendant and follower of Herakles.

Dion, (408–354 BCE), tyrant of Siracusa in Sicily, who was banished by Dionysius II, the son of his brother-in-law, Dionysius I. Returning to Sicily, Dion conquered Siracusa and attempted to reform Sicily but was assassinated by his followers because of his financial and personal behavior.

Dionysius, Bacchus (Roman), the god of the grape harvest, wine, merrymaking, fertility, theater, and ritual madness.

Dis, see Hades.

Ditylas, Sceblyas, and Pardocas, Scythian or Thracian names, perhaps referring to the Scythian slaves who acted as police in Athens.

Earth-Shaker, see Poseidon.

Elis, probably a poetic form of Eleusis, the Greek Sacred Way leading from Eleusis to Athens.

Elpenor, the youngest comrade of Odysseus. On the island of Circe, he drinks too much, sleeps on a roof, and falls in the morning, breaking his neck. Odysseus meets him in Hades.

Elysium, or Elysian Fields, located on the western edge of the earth, the destination for the souls of good humans. See also the Isles of the Blessed.

Empusa, a Greek demigoddess, later taking the form of a monster or specter.

Er, a soldier whose otherworld journey is included in the *Republic* of Plato. Since Er refused to drink the waters of

LETHE — HADES' river of forgetfulness — his body did not decompose, and after two days he revived to report on the matters of the afterlife, including punishment, reward, and reincarnation.

Erebus, a primordial Greek god, the personification of darkness, born to CHAOS. In Greek literature it is also used as the name for the underworld and is occasionally used interchangeably with TARTARUS. With NYX, he fathered personified deities such as HEMERA, HYPNOS, and THANATOS.

Erinys, in Greek mythology, the FURIES.

Eriphyle, a mythic Greek woman who was bribed with rich presents to send both her husband Amphiaraus and son Alcmaeon into war against Thebes. Her son, having promised his father to avenge him, slayed his mother for her treachery.

Eurydice, a Greek nymph or daughter of Apollo and wife of Orpheus. Although there are various versions of her story, in the most often cited, after her death Orpheus traveled to the underworld to release her, but failed when, against the conditions placed on him, he turned back to look at her.

Evadne, in the *Aeneid*, is probably the wife of the blasphemer Capaneus. ZEUS struck him dead during the siege of Thebes, and Evadne threw herself on his funeral pyre. In Greek mythology there are also several others by this name.

Ferryman, see CHARON.

Furies, Erinys, in Greek mythology, the infernal female demons of vengeance: Tisiphone, Alecto, and Megaera.

Gaia, in Greek mythology, the primordial deity and personification of Earth, the mother of all life.

Ganymede, a beautiful mortal or divine hero from Troy. He was abducted by ZEUS, in the form of an eagle, and brought to OLYMPUS to serve as cup-bearer.

Geryon, a monster with three human heads — either on one or three bodies — who dwelt in the western Mediterranean.

Glaucon, brother of Plato and his interlocutor in the *Republic*.

Gorgons, in Greek mythology, three sisters — Stheno, Euryale, and MEDUSA — whose hair was made of living snakes and whose horrid faces turned anyone who looked on them to stone.

Gyes, see BRIAREOS.

Hades, Aidoneus, ancient Greek god of the underworld, ruler over the dead. Later known as Pluto or Dis or Dis Pater. The word also refers to the underworld itself.

Harpies, in both Greek and Roman mythologies, were vicious, vile, and cruel monsters with the bodies of birds and the faces of women. They snatched food from evildoers and abducted them to their punishments in the underworld.

Hebe, in Greek mythology, the goddess of youth, daughter of ZEUS and HERA, cup-bearer on Mount OLYMPUS, wife of HERAKLES.

Hecate, Greek goddess of magic and protective goddess of the family.

Hegelochus, a Greek tragic actor forever remembered for an infamous slip of the tongue at the Great Dionysia drama festival of 408 BCE.

Hektor, also Hector, the greatest Trojan warrior, son of King Priam and Queen Hecuba, husband of Andromache, killed by ACHILLES.

Hemera, the Greek personification of Day, who rarely appears. She is the daughter of NYX and EREBUS, sister of THANATOS and HYPNOS.

Hera, Greek goddess of women and marriage, childbirth and family, married to her brother ZEUS.

Herakles, Heracles, Alcaeus (Greek); Hercules (Roman), Alcides. God of strength, health, and fertility with many well-known stories embellishing his life.

Hermes of Cyllene, Slayer of Argus, Greek god of trickery, messenger of the gods, and guide to the underworld, he is the son of ZEUS, born on Mount Cyllene in Arcadia.

Herodotus, Greek historian (c. 484–25 BCE), from Helicarnassus in Persia, author of *The Histories* on the Greco-Persian Wars.

Hipponax, a Greek poet known for his witty, abusive, and vulgar style.

Homer, semi-legendary Greek poet, author of the *Iliad* and the *Odyssey*.

Hydra, also Lernaean Hydra, a many-headed serpentine monster found in both Greek and Roman mythology who guards the entrance to the underworld.

Hypnos, the Greek personification of Sleep, who rarely appears. He is the son of NYX and EREBUS, brother of THANATOS.

Iapetus, in Greek mythology, a TITAN, son of Uranus and GAIA, who dwells in TARTARUS.

Ida, in Greek mythology, the Mountain of the Goddess Cybele. While there were two Idas, the *Iliad* refers to the mountain in western Anatolia (Turkey), not the other on Crete, where ZEUS was protected in the DICTAEAN CAVE after his birth.

Iris, Greek goddess of sea and sky, personification of the rainbow, and messenger of the gods.

Irus, the nickname of an inhospitable beggar named Arnaeus who ran errands for Penelope's suitors and fought with the returning ODYSSEUS.

Isles of the Blessed or Blest, also known as the Fortunate Isles. A location in the Atlantic Ocean — or sometimes west of the Italian peninsula — where the heroes of Greek mythology might dwell, particularly after repeated reincarnation. It also more generally became the destination of the dead who were favorably judged after death. The isles are associated with CRONOS. See also ELYSIUM.

Ixion, a king of the LAPITHS, bound eternally to a burning solar wheel in TARTARUS for his treachery.

Jove, see ZEUS.

Jupiter, see ZEUS.

Lacedaemon, the Greek city-state of Sparta on the Peloponnese.

Laertes, in Greek mythology, the father of Odysseus.

Laodamia, the wife of the Protesilaus, a Greek hero of the *Iliad* and one of the suitors of Helen of Troy. Upon his death, Laodamia commits suicide.

Lapithae, the Lapiths, a tribe of Thessaly in Greek mythology.

Lethe, one of the five rivers of the Greek underworld, described as the river of oblivion, forgetfulness, unmindfulness, or concealment.

Leto, a daughter of Titans, mistress of Zeus, and the mother of Apollo and Artemis.

Leukas, or Lefkada, a Greek Island in the Ionian Sea between Corfu and Cephalonia.

Love, god of, see Cupid.

Medusa, a mortal Gorgon who was slain by Perseus, who gave her head to Athena to mount on her shield.

Menippus, a satirist of the Cynic School of Greek Philosophy. None of his works survive.

Minos, king of Crete, son of Zeus and Europa, brother of Rhadamanthus. Every nine years Minos required seven Athenian boys and girls to be sent into the labyrinth and eaten by the Minotaur. Minos became a judge of the dead in the underworld.

Mithrobarzanes, described in Lucian's *Menippus,* as a wise and wonderful Chaldean; he was white-haired, with a long imposing beard.

Morsimus, a tragic poet, regarded by some as quite bad. He was a eye doctor, great-nephew of Aeschylus the dramatist, and son of Philocles. He is reported to have written a hundred plays.

Mnemosyne, in Greek mythology, the personification of memory. She is overseer of a pool or lake that is the counterpart to Lethe, the river of forgetfulness.

Nauplius, in Greek mythology, perhaps the founder of the city of Nafplio or the son of POSEIDON and the father of Palamedes. Nauplius the ferryman is unknown.

Neptune, the Roman god who is the counterpart of the Greek POSEIDON.

Nero (15 December 37 BCE–9 June 68 CE), Roman emperor 54 to 68 CE, generally renowned as a tyrant.

Nicander, of Colophon, a Greek poet, physician, and grammarian of the second century BCE. His longest surviving poem, *Theriaca,* is on the nature of venomous animals and the wounds they inflict.

Night, see NYX.

Nireus, one of the Greek suitors of Helen of Troy and second most handsome among the Greek warriors after ACHILLES.

Obriareos, see BRIAREOS.

Oceanus, Oceanos, Okeanos, Ocean, a river or the sea. Also a Greek and Roman god of the sea, a TITAN.

Odysseus, Ulysses in Latin, legendary Greek hero of the TROJAN WAR and the subject of HOMER's epic, the *Odyssey.*

Okeanos, see OCEANUS.

Olympus, the home of the gods in Greek mythology, and actually the highest mountain in Greece, located on the border between Thessaly and Macedonia.

Orion, the great hunter of Greek mythology and the personification of the constellation of the same name.

Orpheus, in Greek mythology, a renowned poet and musician and the prophet of the Orphic mysteries. See also EURYDICE.

Pamphylia, a region in southwest Anatolia, on the Mediterranean coast facing Crete to the south.

Panopeus, a Greek city, approximately 7.5 miles east of Mount Parnassus.

Pardocas, see DITYLAS.

Pasiphaë, daughter of the Sun, Helios. She mated with a bull to give birth to the Minotaur. See also MINOS.

Patroklos, beloved comrade of ACHILLES, killed by HEKTOR during the siege of TROJAN WAR.

Peleus, a Greek hero and the father of ACHILLES.

Penelope, wife of ODYSSEUS, who waits for his return from the TROJAN WAR, while besieged by suitors.

Persephassa, see PERSEPHONE.

Persephone, in Greek mythology, daughter of ZEUS and DEMETER, goddess of the underworld, wife of HADES, as well as a fertility goddess of flowers, spring, and vegetation.

Phaeacia, the island of Scheria in Greek mythology, ruled by King ALCINOUS. ODYSSEUS's last stop before returning to Ithaka.

Phaedra, in Greek mythology, the wife of THESEUS, who was incited by her lies to kill Hippolytus, his son by another woman.

Phlegethon, or Pyriphlegethon, one of the five rivers of the Greek underworld, sometimes described as a river of fire.

Phlegyas, in Greek mythology, king of the LAPITHAE and father of Coronis, one of APOLLO's lovers. He killed her while she was pregnant with their son Asclepius, after he learned that she had fallen in love with someone else. In revenge Phlegyas burned down Apollo's temple at Delphi and in turn Apollo killed him as well.

Pirithous, king of the LAPITHAE and close friend to THESEUS.

Pluto, see HADES. For "Pluto's ravished Queen," see PERSEPHONE.

Poiné, or Poena, in Roman mythology, the spirit of punishment.

Polus, ancient Athenian philosopher described in the writings of Plato and probably an associate of Socrates.

Poseidon, or Earth-Shaker, the Greek god of the seas and of earthquakes, one of the twelve Olympian gods. see also NEPTUNE.

Procris, wife of Cephalus, who tested her fidelity for eight years. He finally seduced her while he is disguised, although they were eventually reconciled. Later she believed, incorrectly, that he had been unfaithful. He accidently killed her in a hunting accident.

Prometheus, a TITAN of Greek mythology, who stole fire from Mount OLYMPUS for humanity, which he created. ZEUS assigned him eternal punishment for this theft.

Proserpina, Proserpine, Roman goddess equivalent to PERSEPHONE.

Psyche, a Roman mortal beloved by CUPID. She was required to overcome numerous obstacles imposed on her by Cupid's mother, VENUS. Although our selection from Ovid's *Metamorphoses* ends with her lying like a sleeping corpse, she was not dead. JUPITER will pity her, and the gods will grant her immortality.

Pyriphlegethon, see PHLEGETHON.

Pyrrhias, possibly a slave in Menander's comedy *Dyskolos* (317–16 BCE).

Pytho, an ancient name for Delphi.

Ravens, in Aristophanes presumably a sign of absolute ruin.

Rest, a euphemism for Death.

Rhadamanthus, in Greek mythology, son of ZEUS and Europa, brother of MINOS. He was one of the judges of the dead.

Rhodope, in northeastern Greece, part of East Macedonia and Thrace, the area of the eponymous Rhodope Mountains.

Salaminia, one of the sacred triremes (galley vessels) of the Athenian navy, particularly during the Peloponnesian War.

Salmoneus, in Greek mythology, the brother of SISYPHUS. ZEUS struck dead the hubristic Salmoneus with a thunderbolt for daring to imitate him and consigned him to eternal torment in TARTARUS.

Saronic Gulf, or Gulf of Aegina, in Greece, forms part of the Aegean Sea and defines the eastern side of the isthmus of Corinth. It is the eastern terminus of the Corinth Canal, which cuts across the isthmus.

Sceblyas, see DITYLAS.

Shade, the spirit, ghost, or soul of a dead person.

Sibyl, see AMPHRYSIAN PRIESTESS.

Sichaeus, or Acerbas, from Tyre, a wealthy priest of HERAKLES, the husband of DIDO (or Elissa). His brother-in-law, Pygmalion, killed him for his riches, but Dido rescued his wealth and brought it to Carthage.

Sisyphus, in Greek mythology, one of the Titans, the brother of SALMONEUS. His hubris and cunning, always tricking death, resulted in a punishment set by Zeus, which entailed eternally pushing a boulder up a mountain in the underworld only to have it slip back down to the bottom just before he reached the top.

Slayer of Argus, see HERMES.

Sleep, see HYPNOS.

Soli, or Soloi, a city of the northwest coast of Cyprus on the Gulf of Morphu.

Sparta, ancient Greek city-state located in the southeast Peloponnese. Also known as Lacedaemon.

Stygian River, Lake or Marsh, see STYX.

Styx, one of the five rivers of the Greek underworld. It formed the border with Earth. Also a goddess, the daughter of Tethys.

Taenarum, see TAENARUS.

Taenarus, the tip of the middle peninsula on the south coast of the Peloponnese, thought to be an entrance to the underworld.

Tantalus, Greek mythological figure, son of ZEUS, assigned to eternal suffering in TARTARUS for cannibalism and kin-slaying. Fruit and water were always before him, but ever out of his grasp.

Tartarus, a deep abyss below HADES set aside for the punishment of the TITANS, but sometimes the place of punishment for the wicked and especially the incurable wicked.

Tartesian Lamprey, a voracious sea eel from Tartessus, an unknown place in the West, perhaps Cadiz, known for producing monstrous creatures, although some have posited that this means a tasty morsel.

Teiresias, Tiresias, in Greek mythology, the blind prophet of APOLLO at Thebes. ODYSSEUS goes to the HADES to seek his advice on the best route for returning home to Ithaka.

Thanatos, the Greek personification of Death, who rarely appears. He is the son of NYX and EREBUS, brother of HYPNOS.

Thaumas, a sea god of Greek mythology, father of the HARPIES and OF IRIS, messenger of the gods.

Thersites, a Greek soldier during the TROJAN WAR, possibly a commoner.

Theseus, the mythical king of Athens, who encounters the six entrances to HADES as he journeys to claim his birthright.

Thunderer, see ZEUS.

Timon of Athens, a misanthropic citizen of Athens during the Peloponnesian War.

Tisiphone, see the FURIES.

Titans, the second generation of Greek gods who descended from the primordial beings whom they overthrew. After their defeat in the War of the Titans (Titanomachy), the deities of OLYMPUS succeeded them and cast them into TARTARUS.

Tithrasos, a river, perhaps located in Libya where the GORGONS resided or perhaps Tithras, an Attic deme, the home of foul-mouthed women.

Tityus, son of ZEUS, a TITAN slain by Artemis and APOLLO for the attempted rape of LETO and stretched out in TARTARUS where two vultures eat his regenerating liver each night.

Trojan War, the mythological war waged by the Greeks (ACHAEANS) under Menelaus, after Paris, the son of King Priam of Troy, abducted Helen, the wife of Menelaus, from Sparta.

Trojans, the citizens of Troy.

Venus, the Roman goddess of Love, counterpart of the Greek Aphrodite. She is the mother of AENEAS as well as the mother of CUPID by the god Mars.

Withering Stone, the first resting place in the kingdom of the dead. It may be comically related to other stones in Greek literature.

Zeus (Greek), Jove and Jupiter (Roman), the god of sky and thunder. Known also as the Elean Thunderer, Zeus ruled the gods on Mount OLYMPUS.

INDEX

A

Achaeans, Achaea 1, 97, 98, 111
Acheron xiii–xv, xxvi, xxxiv, 19, 34, 35, 43, 59, 75, 97, 99, 100
Acherusia
  Cape of xii
  Lake of xiv, xxviii, 34, 97
  Plain of xxxviii, 88
Achilles xxii, xxiii, 5, 7, 97, 103, 106, 107
Adonis 99
Adrasteia xxxiii, 70, 97
Aeacus vii, xvii, xxvii, 19, 21–23, 26, 28, 59, 89, 97
Aegina 97, 109
Aegisthus, see Aigisthos
Aegyptus 100
Aeneas xvi, xx, xxx–xxxi, 41–52, 97, 98, 111
Aeolus 77
Aeschylus 105
Aetna 75
Agamemnon 7, 88, 97
Age xvii, xxx, 42, 58
Aiakos 5, 97
Aidoneus 85
Aigisthos 7, 97
Ajax 7, 97
Alcides 45, 98. See also Hercules, Heracles, Herakles
Alcinous 37, 98, 107
Alcmaeon 102

Alecto 102
allegorical figures xvii, xxx, xxxii. See also Disease, Fear, Death, Famine, War, etc.
Aloïdae 49, 98
Amphiaraus 102
Amphilochus 67, 98
Amphitryon xxxii, 57–60
Amphrysian Priestess 98
Anatolia 99, 104, 106
Anchises xvi, xxxi, 44, 51, 97, 98
Andromache xxii, 103
Antilochos 7, 98
Aornos 41
Aphrodite 111
Apollo 23, 76, 98, 100, 102, 105, 110
Apuleius
  Golden Ass xii, xiv, xxxv–xxxvi, 79–82
Archelaus 30, 98
Archeron, see Acherusia
Archilochus, the poet 75, 78
Ardiaeos the Great xxx, 38–39, 98
Arete 98
Aridaeus xxxiii, 69. See also Thespesius
Aristeides 31, 98
Aristippus of Cyrene xxxviii, 87, 98
Aristophanes 99, 108
  The Frogs xiv, xviii, xx, xxv–xxvi, 15–23

Armenius 37, 98
Artemis 98, 100, 105, 110
Asphodel, Field of xv, xxiii, 5, 91
Athena 6, 99, 105
Athens xii, xxv, 99, 101, 110
Atlantic Ocean 104
Atreus 97
Attic priests 63
Auge of Arcadia 76
Avengers 86
Avernus xii, 48, 54, 97, 99

B

Bacchus 21. *See* Dionysius, the god
Bede, Venerable
   Vision of Furseus xxxiii
Belides xxxii, 54, 99. *See also* Danaides
Boetia 91
Bondage xxx
Briareos (Briareus) xxiv, xxx, 9, 11, 43, 99
Brimo 91
Buddhist hells xx, xxxvi

C

Cadmeids 60
Caeneus 47, 99
Callicles xxvi, 28–30, 99
Callimachus xi
Callisto 77
Capaneus 102
Care 42
Carian 89
Carians 76

Carthage 101, 109
catabases xx
Catania 75–76
Centaurs xxx, 61, 99
Cerberia 16. *See also* Cerberus
Cerberus vii, xiii, xvi, xxiv, xxv, xxxi, xxxii, xxxv, xxxvii, xxxviii, 6, 10, 19, 24, 45, 61–63, 81, 82, 85, 88, 91, 99
Ceres 63
Chaos 11, 42, 102
Charidas xi
Charon, ferryman vii, xiii, xvi, xxv, xxx, xxxii, xxxiv, xxxv, xxxvii, 43, 44, 61, 66, 75, 81, 82, 86, 92, 99
Chimera xxx, xxxviii, 43, 87, 88, 99
Cilicians 67, 99
Cinesias 16, 99
Cinyras xxxvi, 83, 99
Circe xx, xxii, 3, 100, 101
Cleoboea 75
Cleon 20
Clytemnestra 97
Cocytus xiv–xv, xxvi, xxviii, xxxii, xxxv, 19, 35, 43, 44, 58, 64, 79, 97, 100
Corinth xii
Cottus xxiv, 9, 11, 99
Crete xxvi, 48, 59, 101, 104, 105, 106
Cronos xxvi, 27, 97, 100, 104
Ctesias of Cnidus xxxvii, 84, 100
Cumae 98, 99

Cumaean Sibyl. *See* Amph-
    rysian Priestess
Cupid xxxv, 79, 100, 108, 111
Cybele 104
Cyclades 100
Cyllene 7, 103
Cymopolea 11, 100
Cyprus 99, 109

D

Danaans 1, 7, 100
Danaides 60, 100
Danaus 100
    his daughters. *See* Danaides
Dariuses 89
Datis the Persian 76
Day 10
Death xxiv, xxx, 10, 42, 108,
    110. *See also* Thanatos
death, foreknowledge of
    xxvi–xxvii
Delians 76
Delium 76
Delos 23, 100
Delphi xxxiv, 108
Demeter xxiv, 23, 75, 101, 107
Demeter, Hymn to xxiv, 13
demons xvi, 76, 102
despots, kings, tyrants, poten-
    tates xx, xxvii, xxviii,
    xxix–xxx, 29, 30, 38–39,
    50, 60, 88, 98, 101, 106
Dictaean Cave 97, 101, 104
Dido xvi, xxxi, 47–48, 101,
    109
Diké xix, xxxiii, 70, 101
Diogenes 89–90

Diomus 101
Dion xxxviii, 87, 101
Dionysius of Sicily (Syracuse)
    xxxviii, 87, 101
Dionysius, the god 101
Dionysus, citizen of Athens
    xx, xxv, 15–23
Dis xvi, 57, 59, 61, 62, 103. *See
    also* Pluto; *See also* Ha-
    des: god
    Hall of. *See* Hades: Palace or
    Caves of
Disease xvi, xvii, xxx, 42, 58
Dis Pater. *See* Dis
distances xxxi, 1, 9, 33
Ditylas 21

E

Earth 41, 109. *See also* Gaia
Egypt 100
Egyptians xxxviii
Eleusinian mysteries 77. *See
    also* mystery religions
Eleusis 101
Elis 49, 101
Elpenor xxii, 3, 101
Elysium xxxi, 101
    Fields of xvi, xxx, 60, 101
Empusa xxv, 18, 101
Ephialtes 98
Er xx, xxix–xxx, 37–39, 98,
    101–102
Erebus xiii, 3, 13, 102, 103,
    104, 110
Erinys xix, xxxiii, 70, 102
Eriphyle 47, 102
Eumenides 41, 54
Euphrates xxxvii, 85

Euripides xxv
Europa 105, 108
Euryale 103
Eurydice vii, xxxii, 53–55,
    56, 102
Eurylochus 77
Eurynomus xvii–xviii, 76
Eurystheus 63
Evadne 47, 102

F

Fame 54
Famine xvii, 58
Fates. See Erinys
Fear xvi, xvii, xxx, xxxii, 42,
    58
fence of hell 9
ferryman. See Charon, ferry-
    man; See Nauplius,
    ferryman
floors of hell xvi, xxii, 1, 9, 11
Fortunate Isles. See Isles of
    the Blessed
Furies xvi, xxx, xxxi, xxxii,
    xxxvii, 42, 48, 50, 86,
    102

G

Gaia 5, 99, 102, 104
Ganymede 79, 102
gates of hell vii, xiii, xvi, xxii,
    xxiii, xxv, 1, 9, 11, 24
Geryon xxx, 43, 102
ghosts 5–6, 7
giants xvi, 98, 99
Glaucon xxix, 38, 103

Golden Bough xxxi, 45
Gorgons xvi, xxiii, xxvi, xxx,
    6, 19, 43, 103, 105, 110
Great Dionysia, drama festi-
    val 103
Greco-Persian Wars 104
Grief xvii, 58
guides in otherworld xix–xx
Gyes xxiv, 9, 11, 99

H

Hades
  god vii, xvi, xxii, xxiv,
    xxxvii, 1, 3, 10, 12, 13,
    103, 107
  Palace or Caves of xvi,
    xxiv, xxxii, 5, 6, 10, 59,
    80, 85. See also Pluto:
    Palace of
Harpies vii, xvi, xxx, 40, 43,
    103, 110
Hebe 6, 103
Hecate xxxvii, 41, 48, 85, 103
Hecuba xxii, 103
Hegelochus 18, 103
Hekatonkheires 99
Hektor xxii, 2, 103, 107
Helen of Troy 97, 105, 106,
    111
Helicarnassus 104
Helios 100, 106
Hemera 102, 103. See
    also Day
Hera 6, 98, 103
Heracles, Herakles. See Her-
    cules

Hercules, Heracles, Herakles xii, xiii, xx, xxiii, xxv, xxxii, xxxvii, 6, 15, 17, 18, 19, 22, 61–63, 65, 86, 88, 101, 103
Hermes vii, xxiii, 6, 7, 13, *56*, 103
Herod Archelaus. *See* Archelaus
Herodotus xxxvi, 84, 104
Herod the Great 98
Hesiod xi, xiii, xvi, xxxi
 Theogony xviii, xxiii–xxiv, 9–11
Hierapolis xii
Hindu hells xx, xxxvi
Hippolytus 107
Hipponax, poet 23, 104
Hipponium xxvi, 25
Homer xi, xxiii, 27, 33, 78, 88, 98, 104
 Iliad xi, xvi, xxi–xxii, 1–2, 85, 97, 100, 104, 105
 Odyssey xi, xv, xvii, xx, xxii–xxiii, xxxiv, xxxvi, 3–7, 76, 85, 91, 100, 106
Hundred-Arms, the xxiv, 99. *See also* Briareos, Cottus, and Gyes
Hunger xvi, xxx, xxxii, 42
Hydra xxxi, 49, 104
Hyperbolus 20
Hypnos 102, 103, 104, 110. *See also* Sleep

I

Iapetus 10, 104
Ida 1, 104

Idumea 98
Ionians 77
Ionian Sea 105
Iphimedeia 76
Iris 10–11, 104, 110
Irus 88, 104
Isles of the Blessed xxvi, xxvii, 27, 104
Istanbul xii
Italy xxxi, 51
Ithaka xxii, 107, 110
Ixion xxxii, xxxviii, 49, 54, 60, 88, 104

J

Josephus 98
Jove 42, 49, 59
Judea 98
judgment xvii–xix, xxvi, xxxi, 5, 27–33, 35, 37, 39, 46, 59–60
 goddess of 101
 place of xxvii, xxxii
Judgment
 Plain of xv, xvii
Juno xxxii
Jupiter xxxv, 79–80, 108

L

Lacedaemon 105, 109. *See also* Sparta
Laconia. *See* Taenarus
Laertes 3, 5, 6, 105
Laodamia 47, 105
Lapithae 49, 61, 104, 105, 107
Lazio xii
Lebadeia 91

Lerna 43, 61
Lethe xx, xxi, xxvi, xxxi, xxxii, 16, 50, 51, 52, 58, 61, 102, 105
Leto 5, 98, 105, 110
Leukas xxiii, 7, 105
Libya 110
Lucian of Samosata xi, xv, xx
    Menippus xv, xvii, xviii, xix, xxi, xxxvii, xxxvii–xxxix, 85–92, 105
    True History xviii, xxxvi–xxxvii, 83–84
Lysimachus 31

M

Maeander 58
Mars 100, 111
Mausolus 89
Mediterranean Sea 34, 102, 106
Medusa 53, 103, 105
Megaera 102
Menander, Dyskolos 108
Menelaus 97, 111
Menippus xx, 105. *See also* Lucian of Samosata: *Menippus*
Metamorphoses. See Apuleius: *Golden Ass,* Ovid, *Metamorphoses*
Midas the Phrysian 89
Minos vii, xvii, xxvii, xxxi, xxxvii, 5, 26, 28, 46, 59, 86, 87, 105, 108
Minotaur 105, 106
Minyad xxxiv, 75, 76

Mirabilian tradition xii
Mithrobarzanes xx, xxxvii, xxxix, 85, 86, 91, 105
Mnemosyne xxvi, 25, 105
monsters xiv, xvi, xviii, xxv, xxx, xxxv, 15, 17, 51, 61, 79, 80, 103
Morsimus, playwright xxv, 16, 105
Mourning xvii, 58
Mourning, Fields of Sorrow or xv, xxxi, 46
murder xviii, xix, xxviii, xxix, 35
Murder xvii, 58
Mycenae 97
Mylasa 76
Myrrha 99
Mysia 76
mystery religions xi, xxi, xxiv, xxvi, xxxv, 13, 25. *See also* Orphism.
mythological figures xxxiii, xxxiv, 42, 58

N

Nafplio 106
Naiads 53
Naples xii, 98, 99
Nauplius 106; ferryman xx, xxxvi, 83–84
Nausicaa 98
Necessity xxxiii, 70
Neptune 106, 107
Nero 74, 106
Nestor 89, 98
Nicander 74, 106

Night xxiv, 10, 41. *See also* Nyx

Nireus 88, 106

Nyx 102, 103, 104, 110. *See also* Night

O

Obriareus. *See* Briareos (Briareus)

Oceanos. *See* Oceanus

Oceanus xiv, xxii, xxiii, xxiv, xxviii, 4, 7, 10, 11, 34, 106

Ocnus xxxiv, 77. *See also* Sloth

Odysseus xx, xxii–xxiii, xxxiv, xxxv, 3–7, 75, 77, 89, 101, 104, 105, 106, 107, 110

Olympus 1, 11, 49, 98, 102, 103, 106, 107, 108, 110, 111

Orcus xiii

Orion 5, 106

Orpheus vii, xxxii, 53–55, *56*, 102, 106

Orphic Lamina xxvi, 25

Orphism xxii, xxiv, xxvi, 106. *See also* mystery religions

Otus 98

Ovid, *Metamorphoses* xvi, xxxii, 53–55, 99, 108

P

Palamedes 89, 106

Pamphylia 37, 38, 98, 106

Pamukkale xii

Panopeus 5, 106

Pardocas 21

Paris 111

Parnassus 106

Paros 75

Parthian War xxxvii

Pasiphaë 47, 106

Patroklos 7, 107

Pausanias
  Description of Greece xvi, xviii, xxxiv–xxxv, 75–78

Peirithous 75

Peleus 7, 97, 107

Peloponnese xii, 97, 105, 109

Peloponnesian War 108, 110

Penelope xxiii, 7, 104, 107
  her suitors xxiii, 104, 107

Perimedes 77

Persephassa 23

Persephone vii, xvi, xxii, xxiv, xxxvii, 3, 4, 6, *8*, 10, 12, 13, 53, 62, 85, 101, 107. *See also* Proserpina, Proserpine

Perseus 105

Phaeacia 107

Phaeacians, king of the 88

Phaedra 46, 107

Phaiacia 98

Philip of Macedon 89

Phineus 60

Phlegethon xiv–xv, xxviii, xxxi, 34, 35, 42, 48, 97, 107

Phlegyas 50, 107

Phocus 97

Pirithous 6, 45, 49, 107
Pisa 63
Plathane 19–20
Plato xi, xiv, xxi, 98, 107
  Gorgias xv, xvii, xix, xxvi–
    xxvii, 27–31, 99
  Phaedo xiii, xiv, xxvii–xxix,
    xxx, 33–36
  Republic xv, xvii, xviii,
    xix, xx–xxi, xxix–xxx,
    37–39, 101, 103
Platonism xxxiii
Plutarch
  Vision of Thespesius xv, xix,
    xx, xxi, xxxii, xxxii–
    xxxiv, 67–74
Pluto xi, xxvii, xxxvi, 27, 41,
    42, 45, 53, 54, 59, 81,
    103
  Gate of xii
  Palace of xxxvii. *See* Hades:
    Palace or Caves of; *See
    also* Hades: Palace or
    Caves of
Poiné xix, xxxiii, 70, 107
Polus 30, 107
Polycrateses 89
Polygnotus xviii, xxxiv, 75–78
Poseidon 1, 9, 16, 17, 23, 27,
    100, 106, 107
Priam xxii, 103, 111
Procris 46, 108
Prometheus xxvii, 28, 108
Proserpina, Proserpine xxxv–
    xxxvi, 41, 45, 80, 81,
    82, 108. *See also* Perse-
    phone
Protesilaus 105

Protogenes 67, 68
Psyche xii, xxxv–xxxvi,
    79–82, 108
punishment xv, xvii–xix,
    xx–xxi, xxiii, xxv, xxix–
    xxxiv, xxxiii, xxxiv,
    xxxvi–xxxviii, 29–30,
    38, 39, 50, 72–74, 76,
    87–88, 102, 103, 107,
    108, 109–110
  and disfigurement xxxiii–
    xxxiv, 71
  and reparation xxxiii
  extreme xxix, xxxvi, xxxviii,
    30, 60, 71–74, 87
  of friends, relatives and
    acquaintances 72
  place of xv, xvii, xxii, xxxii,
    xxxvi, xxxviii, 83, 87
  purgative power of xv,
    xviii, xxvii, xxxi, 29–30,
    35, 71
  that fits the crime xxxvii,
    52, 59–60, 87
  types of 70–71
Pygmalion 101, 109
Pylos 98
Pyriphlegethon.
    See Phlegethon
Pyrrhias 88, 108
Pytho 5, 23, 108

R

Ravens, the 16, 108
reincarnation xv, xx–xxi, xxi,
    xxxiv, 51, 71, 74, 90,
    102. *See also* souls,
    transmigration of

Rest 16, 108. *See also* Death
Returns 76
Rhadamanthus vii, xvii, xx-
 vii, xxxi, xxxvi, xxxvii,
 26, 28–29, 48, 59, 83,
 85, 91, 105, 108
Rhea 97
Rhodope 53, 108
Rome xxxi
 Lake Curtius xii
Romulus and Remus 97

S

sacrilege xxxiv, 35, 76
Salaminia 17, 108
Salmoneus 49, 108, 109
Samaria 98
Sardanapalus the Assyrian 89
Saronic Gulf xii, 97, 109
Sceblyas 21
Scully Fitzbones of Corpse-
 bury, Cadavershire 90
Scylla xxx, 43
Seneca, *Mad Hercules* xii,
 xiv–xv, xvi, xviii, xxxii,
 57–65
Shade vii, *40, 92,* 109
Shame xvii, 58
Sibyl xx, xxx–xxxi, 41, 42, 44,
 45–46, 48. *See also* Am-
 phrysian Priestess
Sichaeus 47, 101, 109
Sicily 101
Siracusa 76, 101
Sisyphus vii, xxiii, xxxii,
 xxxv, xxxviii, 5–6, *8,* 30,
 54, 60, 77, 88, 108, 109

slaves 101
Slayer of Argus. *See* Hermes
Sleep xxiv, xxx, 10, 42, 58,
 104. *See also* Hypnos
Sloth xxxiv
Socrates xviii, xx, xxvi, xxvii,
 xxvii–xxix, xxix–xxx,
 27–31, 33–36, 37–39,
 89, 107
Soli 67, 109
Sorrow 42
souls xviii, xix, xx, xxi, xxii,
 xxiii, xxvi, xxvii, xxix,
 xxx, xxxi, xxxii–xxxiii,
 3, 4, 5, 7, 25, 27, 28, 29,
 34, 37, 42, 43, 44, 46,
 47, 51, 52, 59–60, 61,
 63, 68–74, 75, 81. *See
 also* reincarnation
 nature of xi
 transmigration of xxxi,
 xxxix
Sparta xxxii, xxxv, 80, 105,
 109, 111. *See also* Lacedaemon
Stheno 103
Strife xxx
Stygian. *See* Styx
Styx vii, xiii–xv, xiv, xxiv, xxvi,
 xxviii, xxx, xxxi, xxxv,
 10, 19, 34, 41, 44–45, 46,
 53, 59, 61, *66,* 79, 80, 85,
 97, 98, 99, 109
Sun 10

T

Taenarus xii, xxxv, 16, 53, 57, 62, 80, 81, 109
Tanagraeans 76
Tantalus xxiii, xxxii, xxxv, xxxviii, 5, 30, 54, 78, 88, 109
Tarquinia xii
Tartarus xiii, xv, xvii, xix, xxii–xxiii, xxiii–xxiv, xxvi, xxvii, xxviii, xxix, xxx, xxxi, xxxii, 1, 9, 27, 31, 33, 35, 39, 49, 53, 59, 65, 97, 99, 100, 102, 104, 108, 109, 110
Tartesian Lamprey xxvi, 19, 110
Teiresias xx, xxii, xxxix, 3, 75, 91, 110
Telamon 97
Tellis 75
Tethys 65, 109
Teuthras 76
Thanatos 102, 103, 104, 110. See also Death
Thasia 78
Thasos 75
Thaumas 10, 110
Thebes 102
theft 108
Theriaca 106
Thersites 30, 88, 110
Theseus xii, xxxii, 6, 45, 57–65, 75, 107, 110
Thespesius 67–74
Thessaly 99, 105, 106
threshold. See gates of hell

Timon of Athens xxxvi, 83, 110
Tisiphone 48, 102
Titanomachy xxiii, 110
Titans xvii, xviii, xxiii, xxxi, xxxv, xxxviii, 9, 11, 49, 51, 99, 100, 104, 105, 106, 108, 109, 110
Titan War. See Titanomachy
Tithras 110
Tithrasos River xxvi, 110
Tityos 60
Tityus xxiii, xxxii, xxxv, xxxviii, 5, 30, 49, 54, 77, 88, 110
Tormentors 86
Trojan War xxi, xxii, xxxiv, 1, 97, 98, 103, 106, 107, 111
Trophonius 91
Troy 48, 97, 102, 111
tyrants. See despots, kings, tyrants, potentates
Tyre 101, 109

U

Uranus 99, 104

V

Venus xiv, xxxv–xxxvi, 79, 80, 81, 97, 100, 108, 111
Vibo Valentia 25
Virgil xiii, 97
    Aeneid xiii, xiv, xvi, xvii, xix, xxx–xxxi, xxxv, 41–52, 102

W

Want xxx
War xvi, xvii, xxx, xxxii, 42,
    58
Withering Stone 16, 111

X

Xanthias xxv, 16–23
Xerxeses 89

Z

Zeus xvii, xxi, xxiv, xxvi–xx-
    vii, xxxiii, 1, 5, 6, 9, 11,
    13, 16, 19, 21, 27, 63,
    70, 76, 97, 98, 100, 101,
    102, 103, 104, 105, 107,
    108, 109, 110, 111

www.ingramcontent.com/pod-product-compliance
Lightning Source LLC
Chambersburg PA
CBHW060402030726
47497CB00003B/826